BEGINNER'S GUIDE TO SKETCHNOTING

FOCUS BETTER, LEARN FASTER, & REMEMBER LONGER BY DRAWING YOUR NOTES

ASHTON RODENHISER

For information contact :
ATG Publishing
info@atgpublishing.com — http://www.atgpublishing.com

Cover and interior design by Chelsea Jewell
Edited by Meg Goodmanson
Photography by Bridget Havercroft Photography

ISBN: 9781738825615

First Edition: June 2023

10 9 8 7 6 5 4 3 2 1

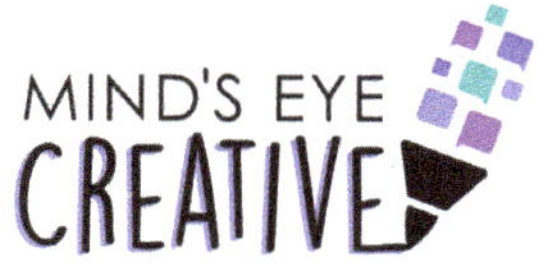

WWW.MINDSEYECREATIVE.CA

To my husband Troy and our amazing children Fern, Aseph & Salix. Thank you for encouraging me to jump in mud puddles, to stop and listen to the birds, and for providing me with a daily belly laugh.

FOREWORD

Hi, I'm Ashton!

Before I discovered sketchnoting, I worked in facilitation and community development. I'd always thought of myself as creative, but I hadn't really drawn anything in years.

Then one day I attended a workshop about graphic facilitation—using sketchnoting techniques to lead meetings in a clear and inclusive way. I didn't really know what sketchnoting was, but I thought it looked interesting.

Little did I know that this one workshop would change the whole direction of my life.

The very next day, I began to experiment with what I'd learned. I found that using sketchnoting to record and facilitate conversations made my work more engaging and powerful. For the next few years, I slowly built my skills and was blown away by how sketchnoting could support not only my own learning but also the learning of others.

I launched a graphic recording and graphic facilitation business called Mind's Eye Creative in 2014. Since then, I've professionally drawn over 2000 presentations and conversations. I routinely capture complex, industry-specific ideas using sketchnoting techniques, and I've recorded graphics for national and international organizations, including Amazon, Microsoft and Michelin.

I've been on the journey I'm about to take you on—and this book is packed with information I've learned along the way!

LET'S GO!

TABLE OF CONTENTS

INTRODUCTION

What is Sketchnoting and Why is it Awesome?

They say "a picture's worth a thousand words"—and that's the concept at the core of sketchnoting! Sketchnoting is the art of capturing ideas using quick drawings and important words or phrases. It's useful in any context where you need to retain and understand what you hear.

Instead of rushing to write information down word for word (which is impossible), you can learn to process the information you hear and create a combination of text and images that contains the key messages. The images support the words and help make the meaning clear.

But what if you always get picked last when deciding Pictionary teams? What if you "can only draw stick figures" (if I had a nickel for every time I've heard *that* one!).

Here's the thing: even though kids are natural artists, by the time we reach adolescence, many of us have lost our confidence. We get caught up in ideas of "good" and "bad." And trust me, I feel that. In grade four, my teacher told me I was drawing "wrong"—and from that point on, I put the marker down and didn't draw much at all... until I found sketchnoting.

I'm here to tell you that we can take our power back and joyfully draw however we want. No matter what anyone else has told us. And we can use those drawings to help us retain and understand the information we record.

Drawing + Information = Sketchnote Magic

Author and visual thinking teacher Brandy Agerbeck has a beautiful philosophy: "Drawing is a thinking tool."[1]

Using drawings to capture ideas disrupts the ways our brains usually process information and forces us to engage with it in new ways. When we do this, we open up fresh perspectives and new connections.

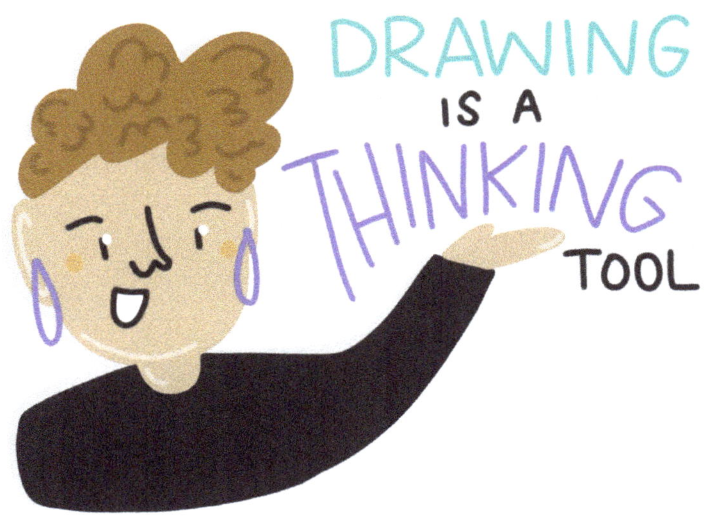

That's why sketchnoting is magic: drawing our notes deepens our relationship with what we're learning. We understand it better and retain it longer than we otherwise would—and *actually retaining* impactful information lets us put our learning into action and create lasting change.

When to Sketchnote

Once you learn to sketchnote, you may find yourself wanting to do it all the time! And that's amazing! Sketchnoting isn't *just* for classes and meetings.

Here are some other contexts where you might want to sketchnote:

- ☑ Reviewing notes you've already written (sketchnoting old notes can help you gain new insights and understanding)
- ☑ Reading a book (sketchnoting can help you remember characters and plot lines)
- ☑ Attending online seminars
- ☑ Listening to a podcast
- ☑ Watching an educational video
- ☑ Fleshing out an idea
- ☑ Basically, any time you're working with information, new or old, sketchnoting can help!

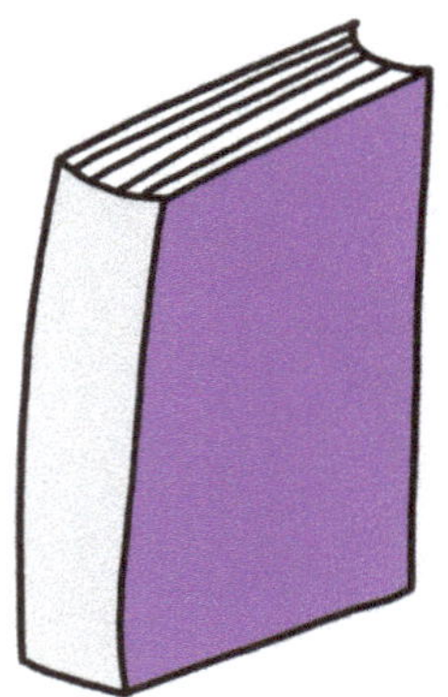
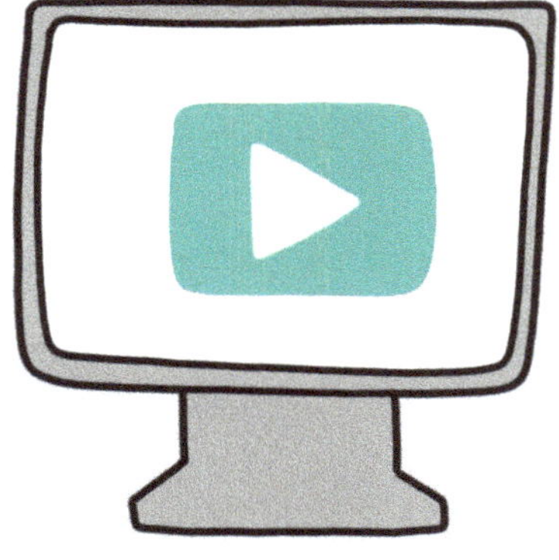
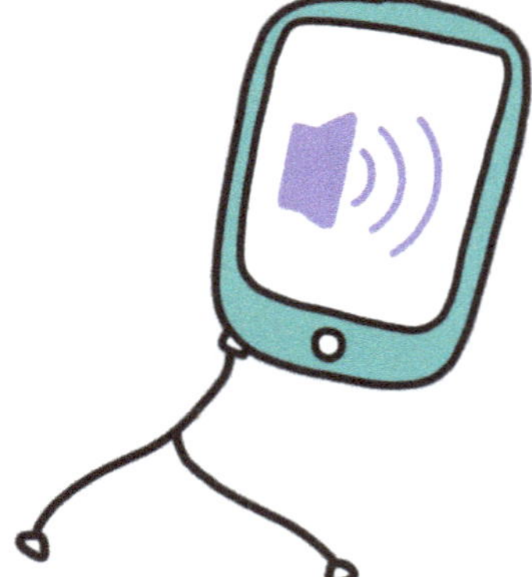

The Science Behind Sketchnoting

There's plenty of research and brain science to support this style of capturing information, and I've scattered some interesting sketchnoting facts throughout the book. Whenever you see this symbol:

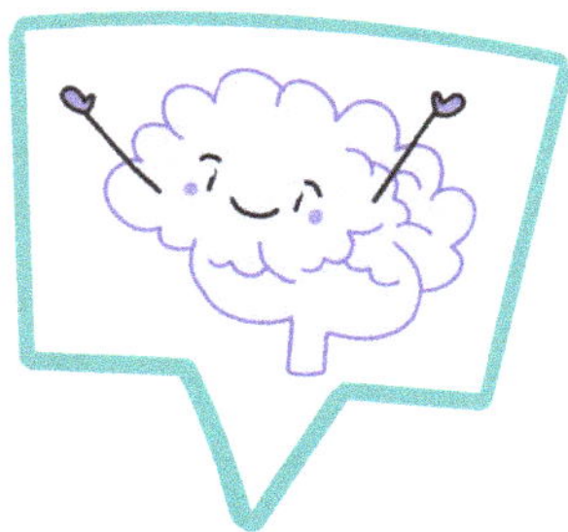

You'll be enlightened by a statistic or study on the benefits of sketchnoting to encourage you to keep going! Want to read more? The original sources are listed in the back of the book.

This Book is for Anyone Who Wants to Learn!

Sketchnoting doesn't discriminate, so no matter your age, background, or preferred learning style, whether you have art experience or not, this book can help you unlock your best opportunities for learning and growth.

Sketchnoting can be especially useful for:
- Visual or kinesthetic learners (people who learn best with a pen or pencil in their hand)
- Frustrated notetakers who struggle to retain the information they write down
- People who want to invite more creativity into their lives

But regardless of how you found this book or why you want to learn this skill, I'm excited to be on this journey with you! If you feel like sharing your progress as you go through the book, use the hashtag #sketchnoteallthethings so that I—and other budding sketchnoters like you—can follow along!

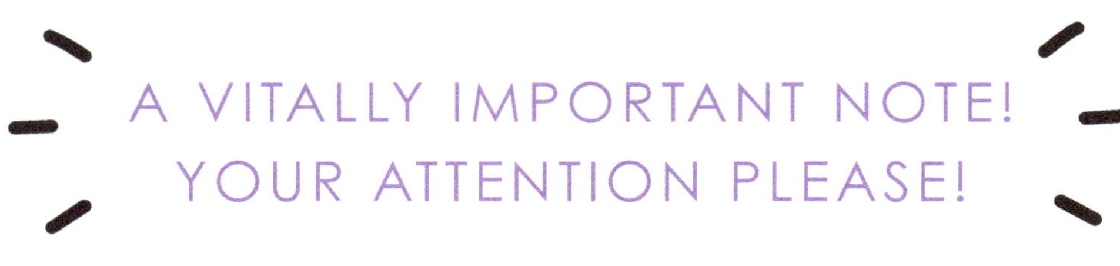

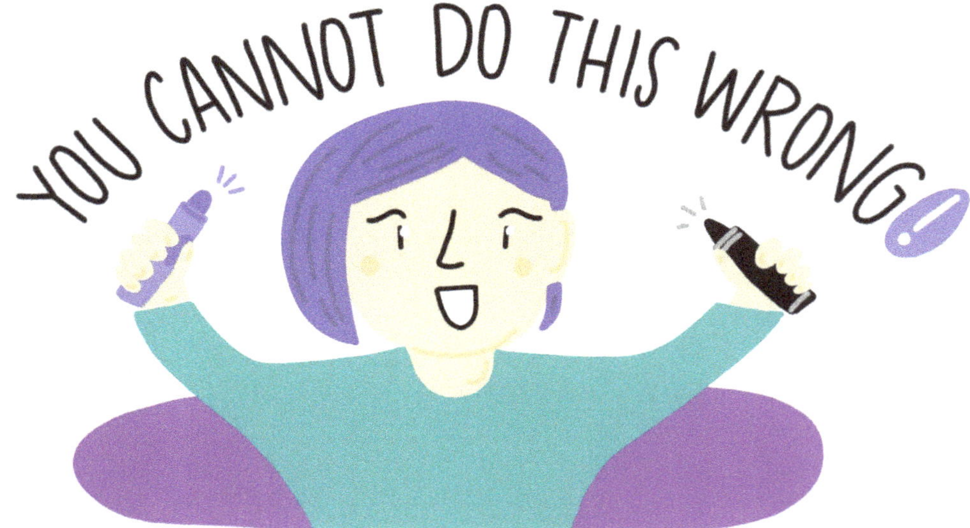

You Can't Do This Wrong (Seriously!)

This book breaks down the different elements that go into a sketchnote and takes you through the process of creating one. It'll set you up for success and build your confidence.

But the most important thing to remember is that there are no wrong answers here. Let yourself PLAY! Do what feels right to you. Follow your intuition!

Sketchnotes are a tool for your personal learning—and that means that they only need to have meaning for *you*. Your sketchnotes may (and probably will) look entirely different from mine. And that's GOOD. Find and embrace YOUR style.

What's in This Book: A chapter-by-chapter sneak peek

This book is a mix of instructions and illustrations to help you digest information quickly. It's important to read it in order—don't skip around on the first read-through. Each step builds on the previous ones, so give yourself time to integrate them.

The first part of the book breaks down all the elements of a sketchnote and shows you how to create and use them. The second part looks at the act of sketchnoting (listening to information, figuring out what to record, and combining all the elements on the page) and gives you tips for success.

By the end of the book, you'll have a solid feel for sketchnoting and have plenty of exercises and experiments to practice with.

Here's a taste of what's in each chapter:

BEGINNERS GUIDE TO SKETCHNOTING

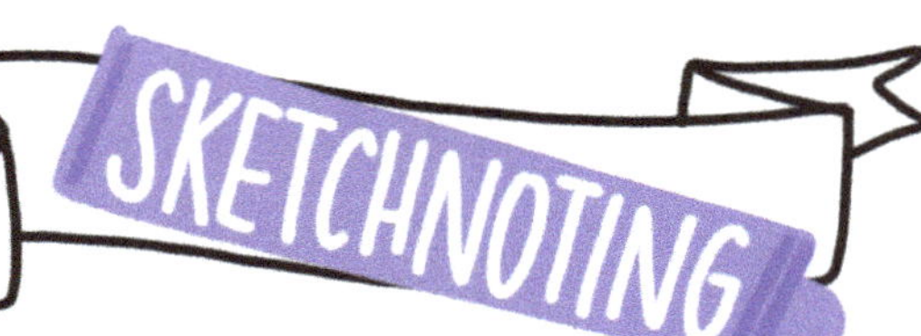

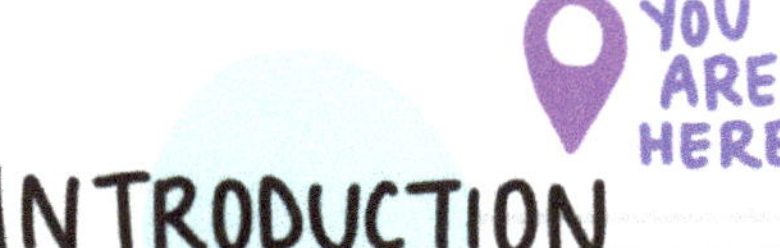

INTRODUCTION

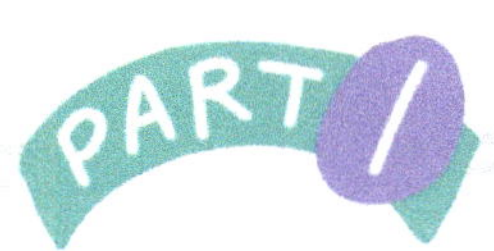

GET STARTED

ENHANCING CLARITY WITH CONTAINERS

CREATING FLOW WITH LINES & ARROWS

LETTERS & WRITING

ABC

DRAWING PEOPLE IS EASY

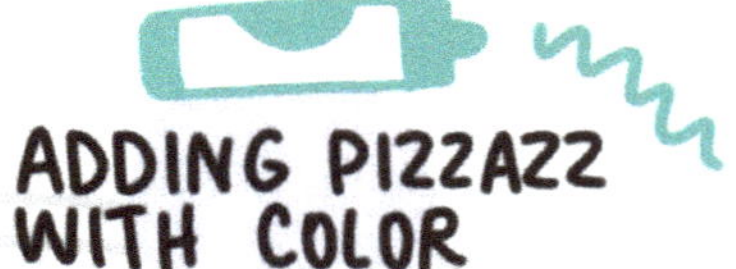

ADDING PIZZAZZ WITH COLOR

INTERLUDE

THE SKETCHNOTING PROCESS

LISTENING

MAKING SENSE

CAPTURING

ONE LAST THING TO REMEMBER

BRINGING IT ALL TOGETHER

SKETCHNOTING USES A VISUAL LANGUAGE & YOU CAN PRACTICE IT!

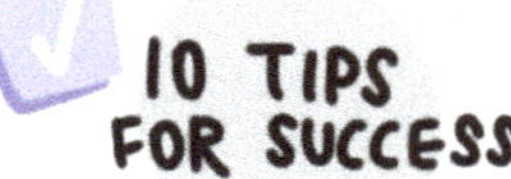

10 TIPS FOR SUCCESS

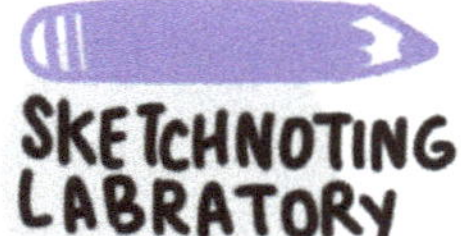

SKETCHNOTING LABRATORY

Go through the material as fast or as slow as you want to! Just make sure to practice drawing at each step. You'll thank me later. Practice builds your muscle memory and hones your instincts, so by the time you've finished the book, you'll already feel your confidence growing.

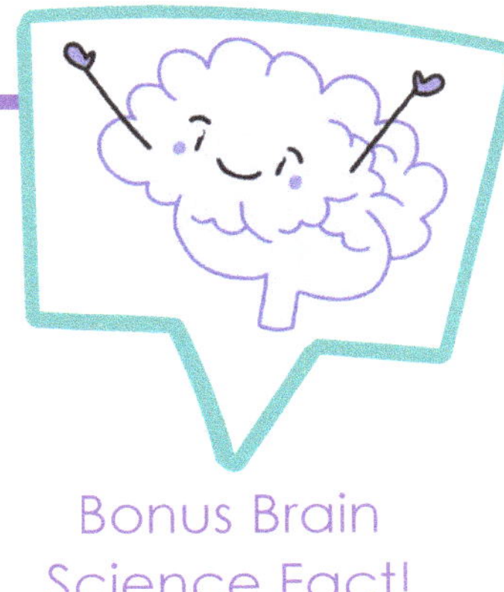

Allan Paivio's Dual Code Theory suggests that students learn better when they experience information in two ways (verbally and non-verbally). By combining images with text, sketchnoting gives the brain two ways to process information. It also requires more active listening because sketchnotes are processing the information in multiple ways as they go.[2]

Custom Graphics and Sketchnote Samples!

Since sketchnoting is a visual medium, I've included all kinds of graphics to inspire you! As you read, you'll find example mini sketchnotes, extensive "cheat sheets," sample exercises, and more!

If you want even *more* inspiration, excellent resources are just a click away! (see my online resource page for my favorites!) You can also look for the hashtag #sketchnoteallthethings on your favorite social media platforms to see what other students have been sharing.

Sketchnoting: A (Brief) History Lesson

The words "sketchnote" and "sketchnoting" were coined by the author of *The Sketchnote Handbook*, designer and illustrator Mike Rohde, back in 2006, but the concepts have been around much longer.[3] We've been using drawings to help communicate ideas throughout history.

Prehistoric people created cave art that preserved a record of events or stories before writing even existed. Football coaches have used whiteboards to draw out complicated plays for decades. Students in classrooms study (and recreate) diagrams of life cycles, water cycles, and anatomy, to name just a few!

The specific techniques we use in sketchnoting originated in the 1970s. There are many related terms, and different people use them in different ways.

Sketchnoting Can Also be Called:

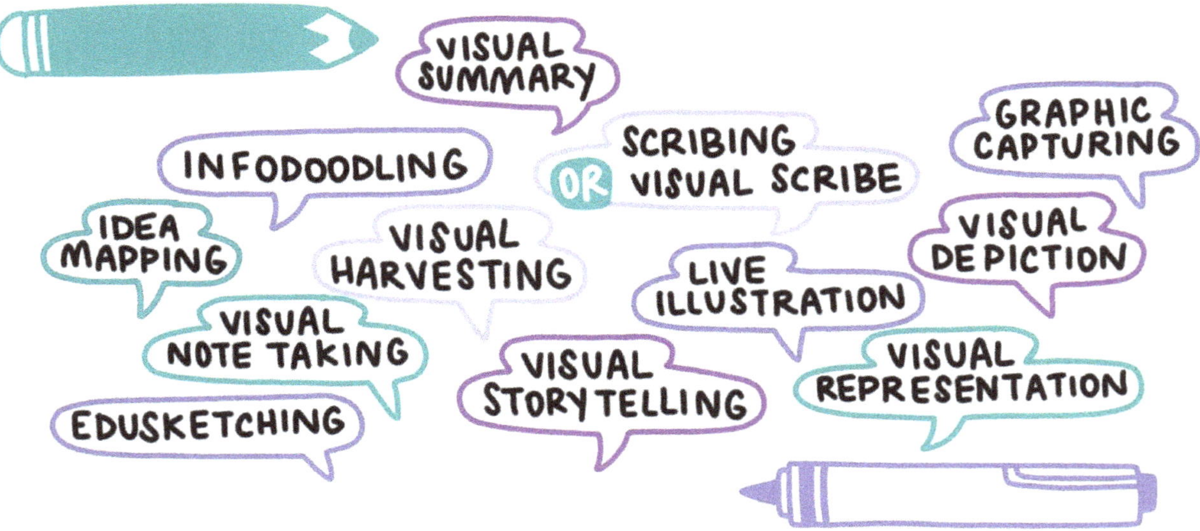

Some of the stories and tips in this book come from my work as a professional graphic recorder and graphic facilitator. In these roles, I use sketchnoting techniques to create images for clients and organizations. There's more to it, of course, but that's the basic idea. You can find more information about professional graphic recording and facilitation in the online resource guide.

Share Your Sketchnotes? (It's Up to You!)

The great thing about sketchnoting is that it's totally up to you if you want to share with others. If people see you sketchnoting, they'll often ask you questions about what you're doing. Sketchnotes can be personal and kept just for you—that's a completely valid choice. As your confidence grows you may choose to share, and that's amazing too.

My hope is that you will share, and share widely, because I know your sketchnotes will make a positive impact on others. Just remember: they're *your* learning tool. If you're nervous about sharing, don't put pressure on yourself, especially in the beginning.

PART ONE

Anatomy of a Sketchnote

When you're starting something new, it's common to feel like you need to go out and buy special supplies in order to do it properly. I'm here to tell you that you absolutely do not need to do this. That voice is perfectionism, and we don't have any time for it here!

In fact, we have so little time for perfectionism that we're going to jump into your first exercise right now! If you're nervous about drawing, don't worry! We aren't even going to get to drawing yet! We're going to take this nice and slow.

For this first exercise, you're going to collect everything you need in order to start sketchnoting.

Ready?

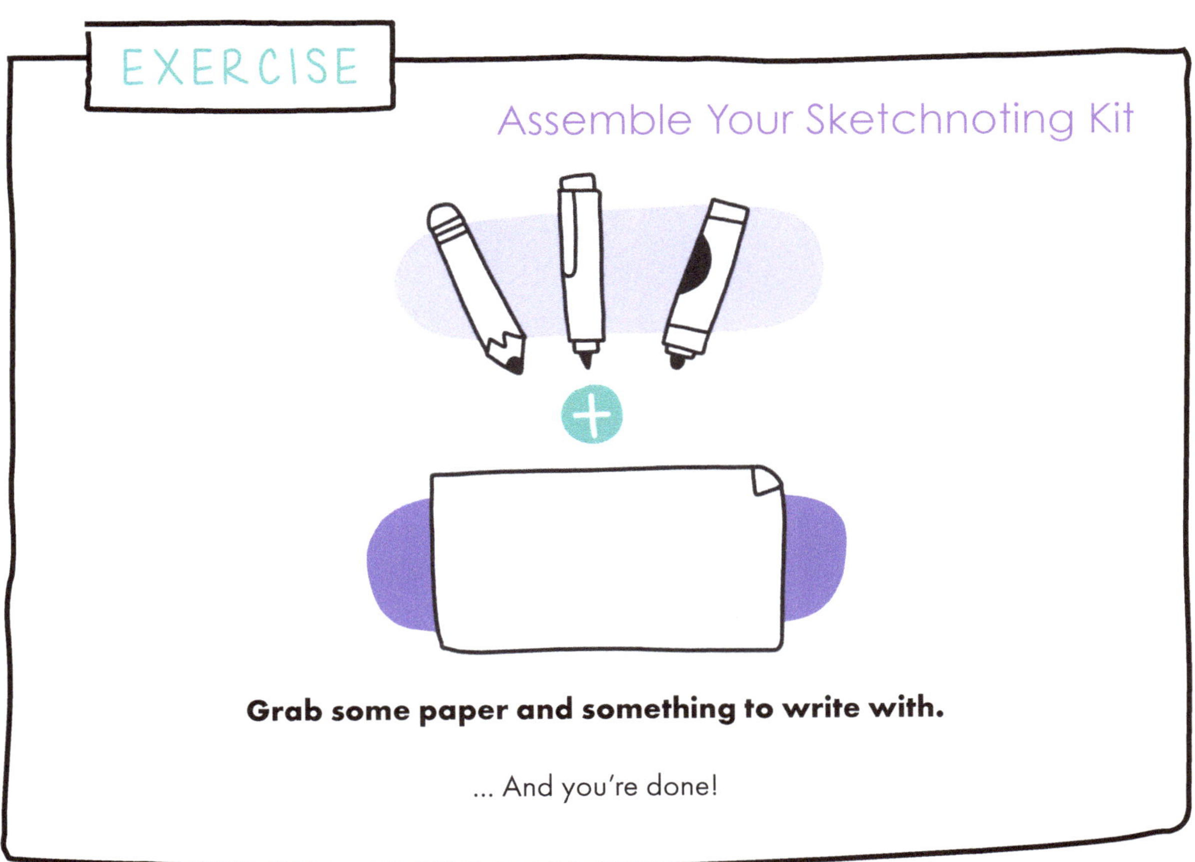

That's it. Seriously. It's one of the things I love the most about sketchnoting.

When people are just starting out, I usually recommend working in pencil because it's easy to erase. But it's honestly up to you. Pens can be great because most people have them on hand already. I personally use markers because I like the softness of the marker tip on the paper. Pick your favorite!

If digital notetaking is your thing, a tablet and stylus also work perfectly. You don't need to go out and purchase a new device for this, but if you already prefer digital, then feel free to stick with digital.

Go with whatever makes you feel good! If you're curious about what I use, I've included some info about my go-to supplies (physical *and* digital) in the resource section.

Use Plain White Paper

The best paper for sketchnoting is blank, white paper, held horizontally. Our brains often default to linear thinking, and lined paper encourages this approach. Blank paper gives you permission to use the space in different ways.

And yes, I know, it can be very intimidating to approach a blank page. I totally get it. Stay with me and we'll get you past that.

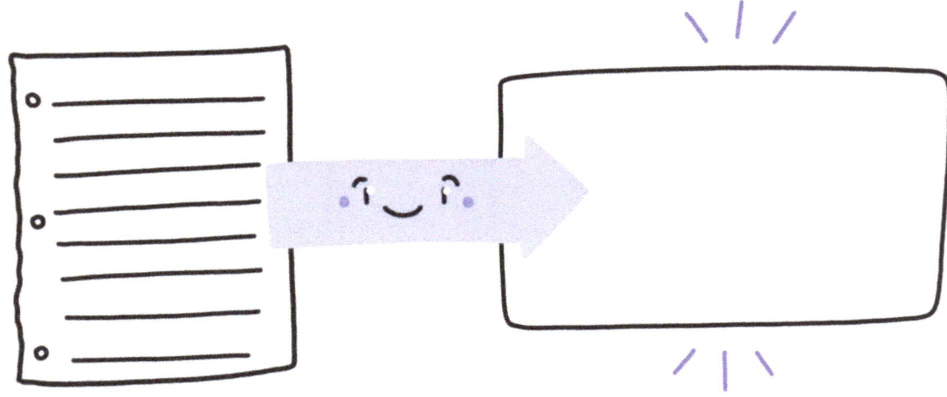

Create Your First Sketchnote While Reading This Book

I've created mini sketchnotes based on the content for steps two through six which you can find at the end of each step, highlighting the elements of that section.

I want you to follow along and create your first sketchnote. You can either:

1. Pick a topic that you know a lot about and use that as your
practice as you go through the steps.

Or

2. If you aren't sure about a topic to do, copy my mini sketchnotes! That way you will be sketchnoting a sketchnote about sketchnoting. How's that for making the information stick?

Overcome the Blank Page With a Title

Before you do anything else, draw a title. Starting with your title can help you build confidence—it's a small thing, but it gets you putting pen to paper. Now you aren't staring at a blank page anymore!

You can put your title at the top, in the middle, or on the side. If you have 5 minutes or more, you can take your time, get in the zone, and get your creative juices flowing with a fun design. You may also only have fifteen seconds to grab a marker and quickly write the presentation title or name of the class—that's totally fine as well!

Don't make the title too big. Keep it to no more than 10 - 15% of your page. Play around with the position of the title and find out where you like it best.

Sticking the date on your sketchnote at this point is also a good habit to get into. It doesn't have to be anything fancy—a tiny note in a corner of the page is just fine.

Dating your sketchnotes is especially useful if you're attending a series of meetings or classes. Just like any notes, you want to be able to put them in order and see how the information develops from sketchnote to sketchnote.

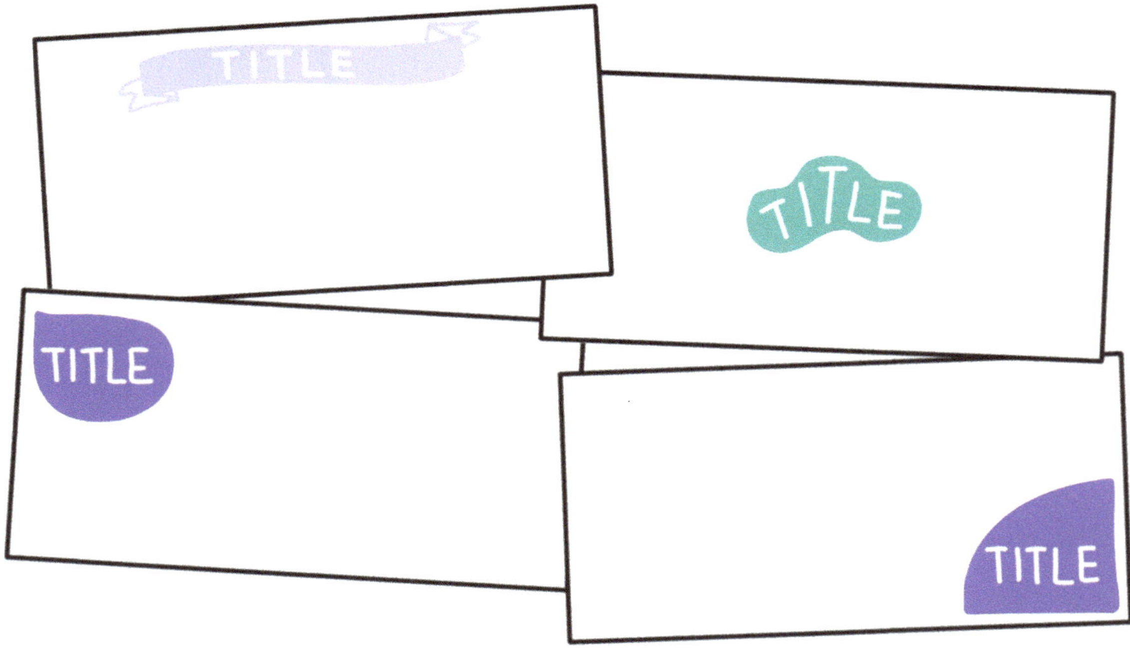

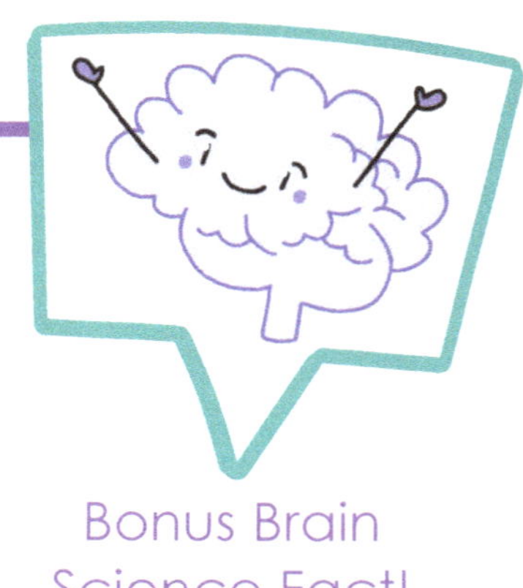

Is sketchnoting distracting? No! A 2009 study in *Applied Cognitive Psychology* found that people who doodled while listening to a list of names retained 29% more information when quizzed later. Sketchnoting combines the benefits of doodling with the benefits of active listening to create a truly powerful tool for focus and information retention.[4]

Choose Your Starting Point

It's totally normal if you feel the urge to capture the information in the same way that you would on lined paper, which is left to right. Overcoming that habit opens up a world of possibility and while it can feel incredibly freeing, it can also feel overwhelming. In the examples throughout the book I write the titles at the top of the page. I often start sketchnoting at the top under the title. But really, you can start anywhere you want.

Every time you create a sketchnote, try starting in a new place on the page and see how that feels. By testing different layouts, you'll likely end up with a preference or two.

A layout is the way you choose to place your information on the page. Where do you want your eyes to go first? How do you want to direct them around the page?

A layout can be really important in a situation where the information presented has a correct order (like a series of events or a set of instructions). In that case, you want your eyes to flow from step 1 to step 2, and so on.

You can start your sketchnote with a general idea of how you want it to flow around the page—or you can make it up as you go along. Either way is totally valid, so don't worry.

Here's some examples of layout flows that you can consider:

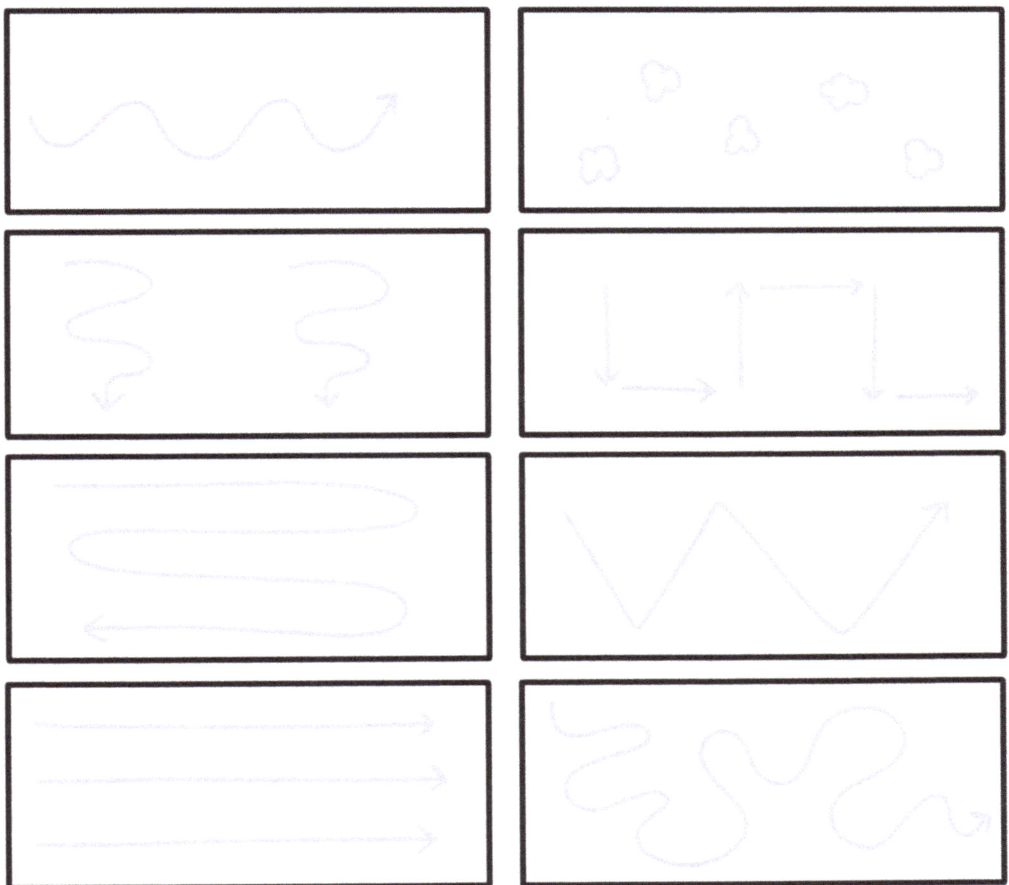

A layout isn't the same thing as a template, which is more structured and usually involves knowing a bit about the material before you begin. A template divides the page into sections in advance, while a layout is a looser, more flexible way of letting information flow onto the page.

I generally find sketchnoting templates to be unhelpful (they're too structured and don't let me freely capture information) so I'm not going to dig further into them in this book. They're easy to find online and I've included some you can download in my online resource guide.

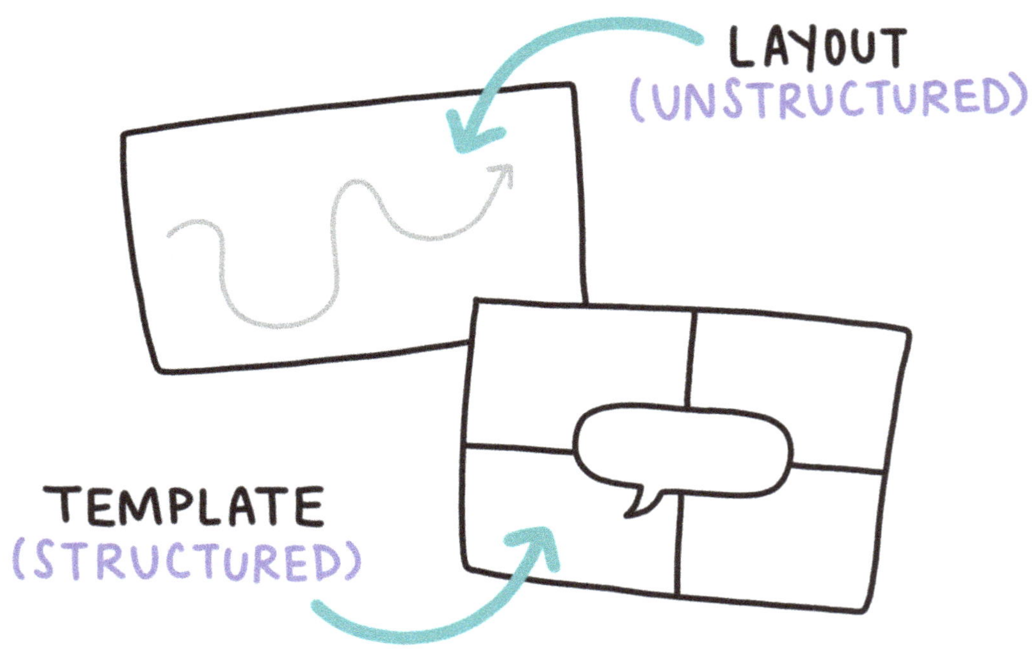

Leave Breathing Space

Breathing space is the unsung hero of sketchnoting! Leaving lots of space in between ideas can make the difference between a crowded, confusing sketchnote and a clear, effective one. Seriously! It's better to have what feels like "too much" breathing space than not enough.

When we leave space, we make sure that we're able to make connections with new information. If we cram ideas too close together then we won't have room for things that might be mentioned later on.

And don't worry about having too much space left at the end—you can fill it in with a drawing that relates to the concept or choose to leave it be. In this graphic below the gray areas represent the empty breathing space.

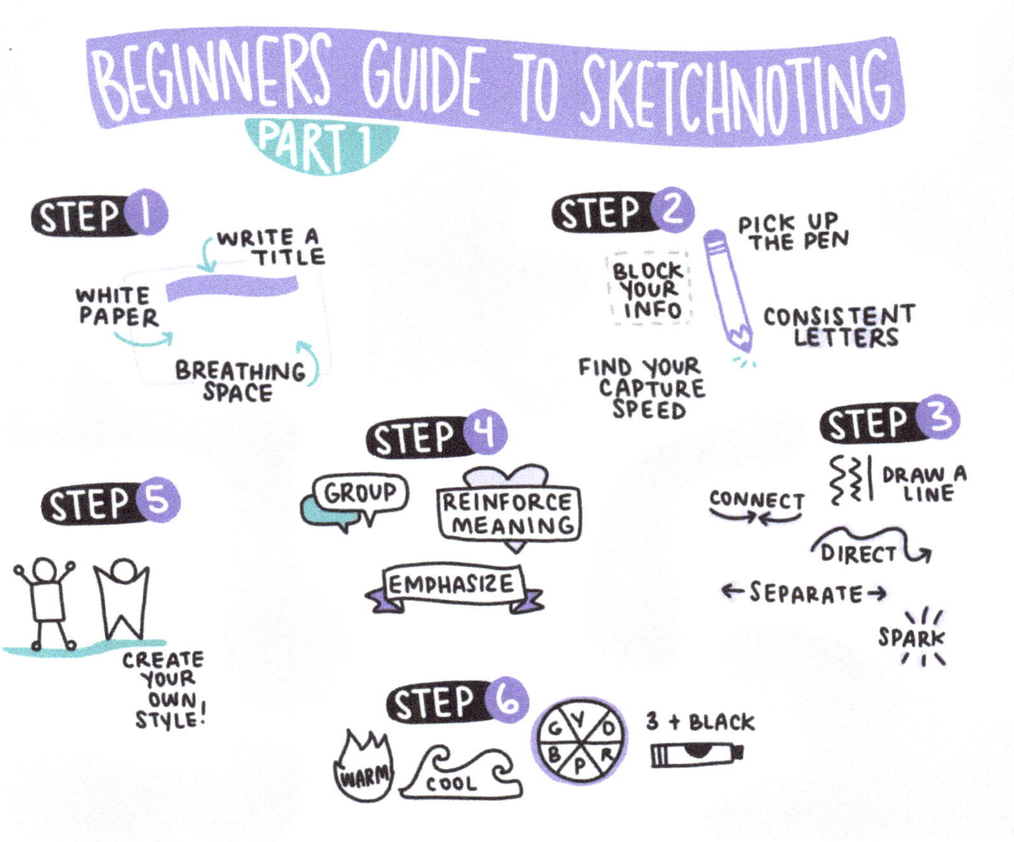

"But Ashton, what if I run out of room?"

I hear this all the time, and I get it. I've included some tips later in the book, but for now, just keep in mind that your information really does need to breathe. You'll get better at managing space as you practice (and in a pinch, you can always add a second page!).

Letters are Drawing in Disguise

Do you hate your handwriting? If you do, that's ok!

Handwriting is just any writing you do with a pen or pencil. You have permission to love it, hate it, or be completely indifferent about it.

Think about writing as drawing in its basic form. If you know how to write, you know how to draw. If you feel like your handwriting could improve, then practice your letter shapes. Write out the alphabet and analyze which letters you don't like. Then practice those until you do.

When you're sketchnoting, I recommend printing your letters for maximum readability.

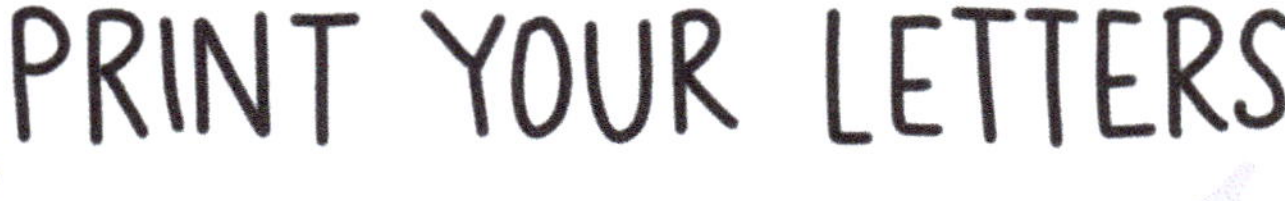

Embrace your own printing style and if you have a classmate or coworker with teacher-perfect handwriting, don't compare yourself to them. This sketchnoting is a tool to help you remember information, so it should feel comfortable to you!

Confession: I'm not a fan of my lowercase letters and haven't spent enough time practicing, so I just don't use them! I've dedicated time to the letters that I do love, which are all uppercase. You don't have to do the same—just do what feels right!

I know you might be wondering WHAT to write when you're creating a sketchnote, but keep going! We'll get into listening tips and deciding what to capture in Part Two. We're simply focusing on the HOW for now. You've got this!

Lift Your Pencil

To make your letters more legible, lift your pencil (or pen, marker, stylus, whatever you're writing with) every time you make a mark. It may feel like it's adding more time and slowing down your writing, but the more you do it, the faster and more legible your writing will be. Lifting your pencil keeps you from running your letters together, which is usually what makes them messy.

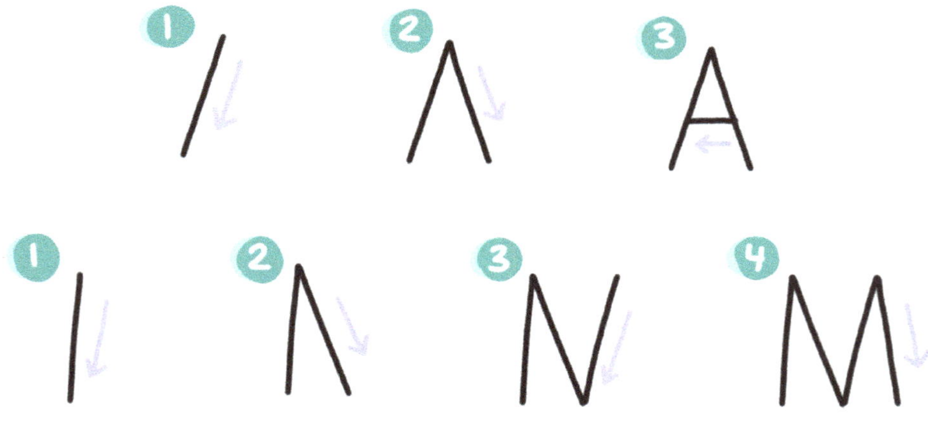

Consistency Will Help Your Writing Look Neater

For a consistent look, try to make each letter the same each time. Take the capital letter "E" for example. If you draw each line on the "E" in a different place each time, when you look at your sentence as a whole it'll look messy even if the letters are drawn neatly.

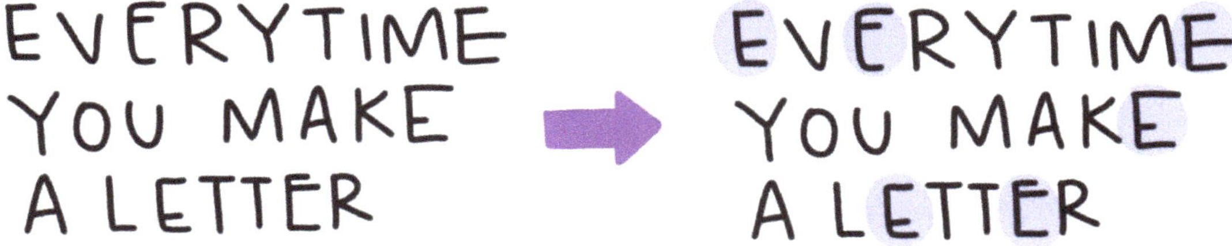

But if you write the letter in the same style, placing each line in roughly the same position and making them all the same length, your sentence as a whole will look a lot cleaner.

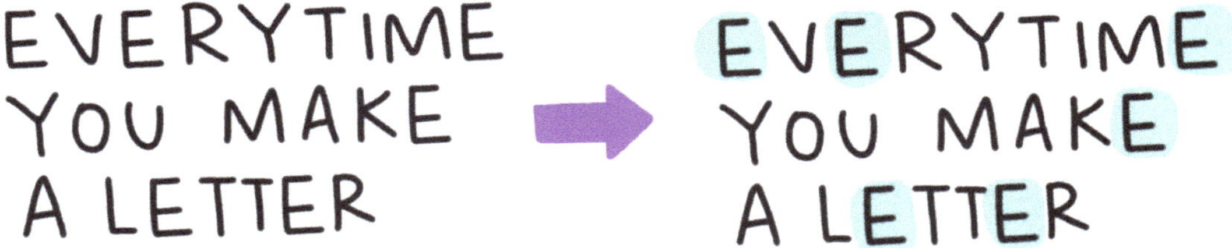

Find your ideal writing speed

How fast can you write without being too messy? On a blank piece of paper, complete the following steps:

1. Write out the alphabet as quickly as you can.
2. Write out the alphabet as slowly and neatly as you can.
3. Lastly, write out the alphabet somewhere in between speed 1 and speed 2.

WRITE FAST

ABCDEFGHIJKLMNO
PQRSTUVWXYZ

WRITE SLOW

ABCDEFGHIJKLMNO
PQRSTUVWXYZ

JUST RIGHT

ABCDEFGHIJKLMNO
PQRSTUVWXYZ

We're looking for an in-between writing speed that allows you to capture information quickly but is still okay to read. You don't want your writing to be illegible later on when you're reviewing your sketchnotes. You also don't want to write so slowly that you start to fall behind and miss vital pieces of information.

Eventually, as you practice writing at this just-right-for-you speed and get more confident with your letters, you'll just naturally get faster while keeping your letter shapes consistent.

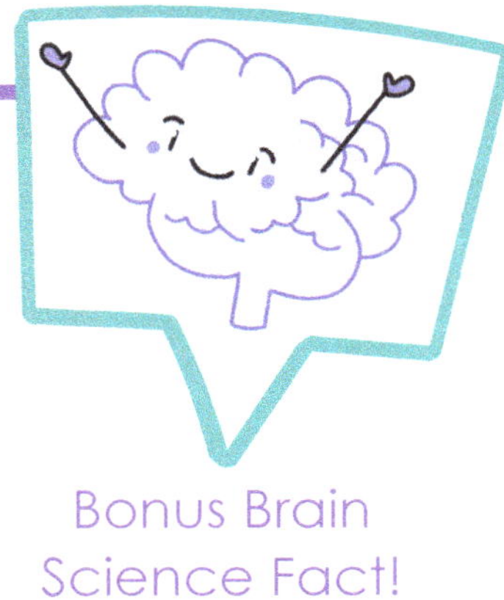

Studies show that on average we speak 2.3 words per second while average note-taking speeds are around 0.3 or 0.4 words per second. That means we're writing 6 to 8 times more slowly than the material we're listening to! No wonder we can't keep up when we try to write things word for word![5]

The Size of Your Writing Has Meaning

This is going to sound obvious, but I'm still going to say it: Change the size of your writing to reflect the importance of the information. The relative importance of information is called hierarchy, and here's the simplest way to show it: Write big ideas bigger. Write smaller ideas normally. Write supporting details smaller.

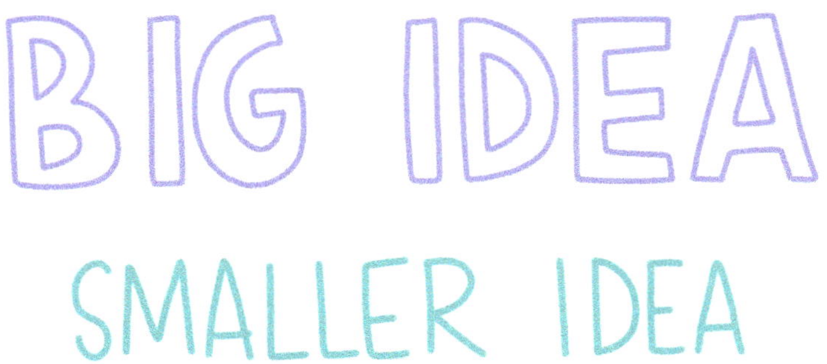

Sometimes you won't know exactly how big to write your information. That's ok! If you aren't sure, you can choose to write everything in similar sizes and use other drawing elements in this book to help you show hierarchy instead of the size of the letters.

You can also use writing style to indicate hierarchy. For example, instead of using the size to show relative importance, you can use capital letters for your larger ideas and lowercase for smaller/ supporting details.

You'll want to keep your available space in mind as well when deciding how big to write something.

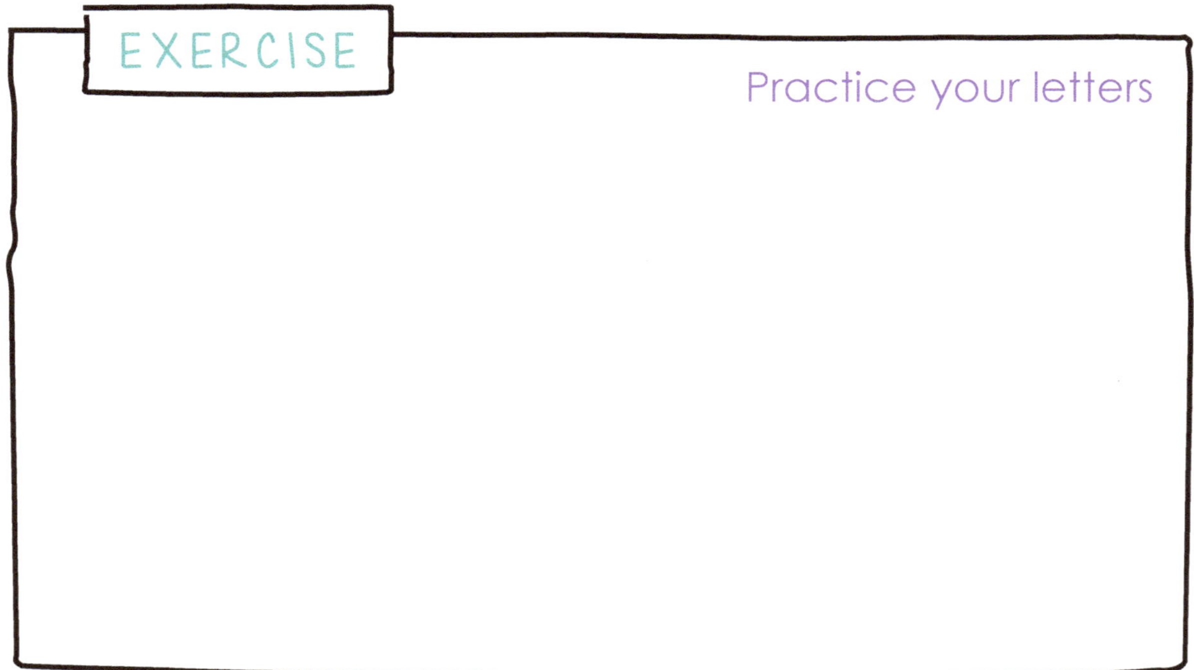

Blocking Your Content

When capturing notes on lined paper, we write sentences that stretch across the entire width of the page and continue onto the next line. But in sketchnoting we're going to switch up how we capture information and use a technique called "blocking."

When you block your content, you write in imaginary boxes (or blocks) instead of long horizontal lines. This way, you end up with smaller, bite-sized bits of information that leave you with plenty of space to put stuff around them. This is a good place to remember the idea of breathing space from earlier—don't cram your blocks too close together!

EXERCISE

Block your content

Practice taking a sentence and putting it in a block. Imagine an invisible box around the information and make your text fit inside of it. It's ok if it's not perfectly square, since words vary in length.

INSTEAD OF WRITING EVERYTHING OUT IN A LONG LINE

TRY TO BLOCK YOUR WRITING IN A SQUARE

When I block my information, I prefer to write my blocks in straight horizontal lines, and not at an angle. I find that angled content can be hard to read and may not allow for you to organically embellish it later.

TEXT LIKE THIS IS A LOT EASIER TO READ

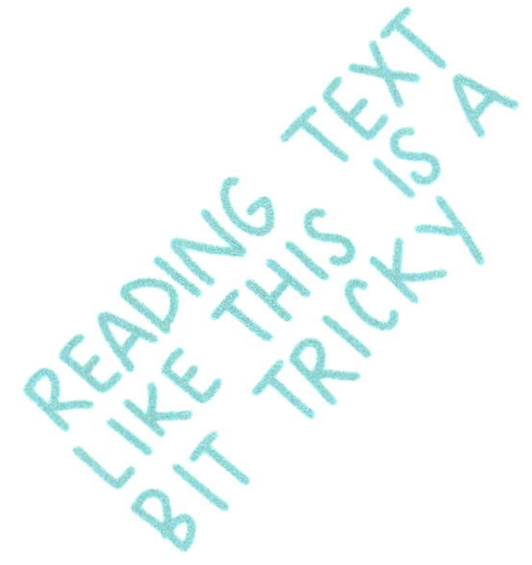

In step four, we'll look at how to use containers to elevate these blocks of information, but for now, just practice writing in an imaginary box.

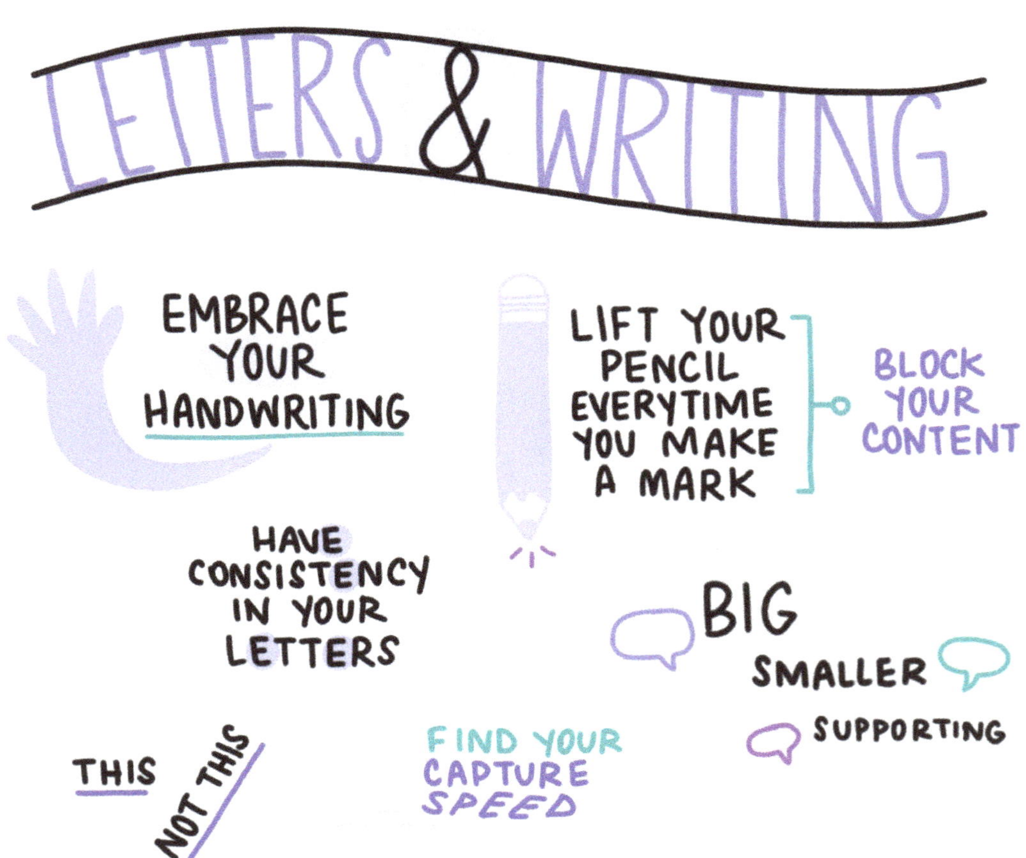

Here's a sketchnote that summarizes Step Two. You can see that I stripped the ideas down to their core message. Don't be afraid to do this. I find that I'm consistently able to remember details beyond what I've captured, and I've had clients tell me the same.

In the next few chapters, you'll learn how to draw some more of the elements that you see here and be able to pick out the different ways they're used.

STEP 3 — CREATING FLOW WITH LINES AND ARROWS

Now that you've got the idea of how to write your information, we're going to look at a couple of elements you can use to create a flow around the page.

A clear flow helps guide your eye from the first piece of information to the last and gives you a sense of progression. It also illustrates how things relate to each other. Two great tools for showing flow are lines and arrows.

Take a Deep Breath ... and Draw a Line

Whenever I tell a group of students about lines and arrows, at least one of them says, "Yeah right, Ashton, I can't even draw a straight line!" I hear it All. The. Time.

And you know what? I have two answers to that:

1. You don't HAVE to be able to draw a straight line! Every single one of your lines could be crooked and it wouldn't make your sketchnote any less useful.

2. But that being said, it never hurts to practice. Getting comfortable with drawing straight lines will build your confidence. It'll also develop the muscle memory to help you draw other types of lines—which will help you draw lots of different things.

Also, I have an easy technique that can help. You could be just a few practice sessions away from NEVER thinking "but I can't even draw a straight line!" again! Really! Take a deep breath. I've got you!

Straight lines ... let's do this.

You Absolutely *Can* Draw a Straight Line, and Here's How

I learned this technique from a watercolor artist who suggested that you use your arm, not your wrist, to draw a straight line. Hold your pencil and pull your arm towards your body, keeping your hand and wrist straight. Now you have your whole body engaged in the process.

You can use this technique to draw straight lines in any direction. Think of your hand, wrist, and arm as a single unit. In art class they call this "drawing from the shoulder."

Practice drawing lines over and over again. You've got this!

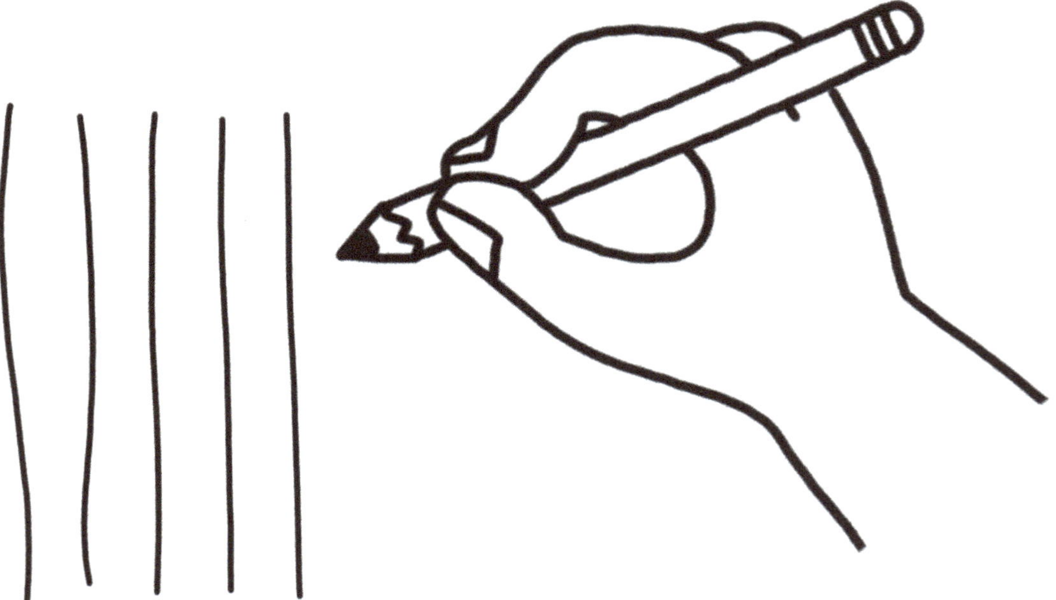

Once you start to feel more comfortable putting pencil to paper, let's get your creativity flowing!

EXERCISE

Explore different lines

Draw a wavy line

Draw a zig-zag line

Draw a dotted line

Draw a dashed line

Draw a loop-de-loop line

Invent your own

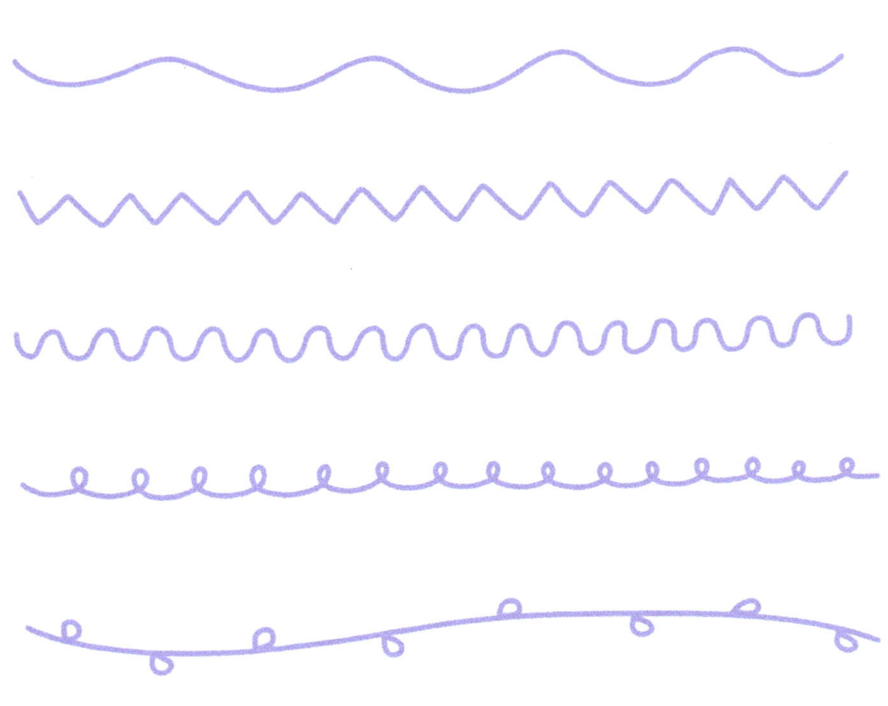

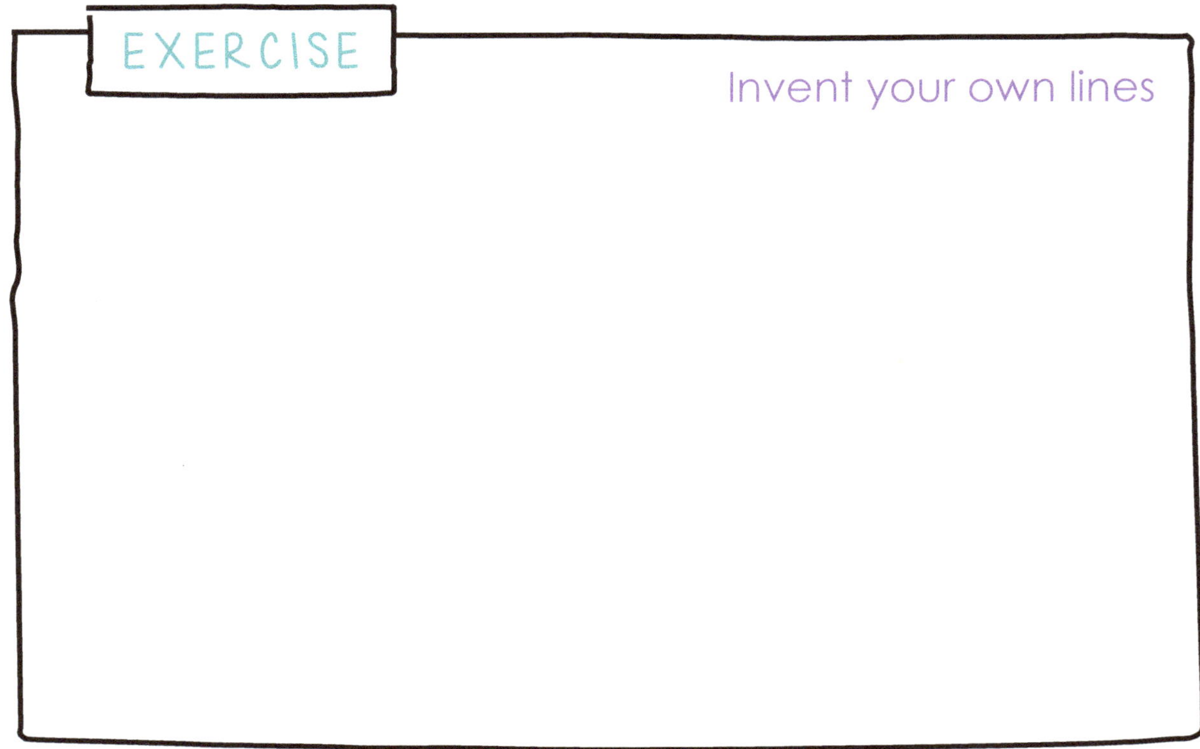

See? What did I tell you? You CAN draw a straight line (and all kinds of other lines as well).

Point Me to the Arrow (Get it?)

Our next drawing element is an arrow. Let's start simple: Draw a line and add a point on the end.

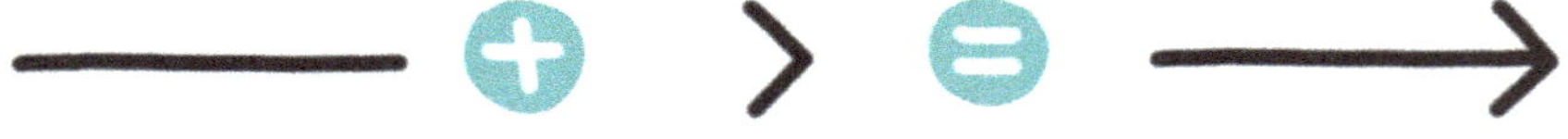

Voilà! You did it! You drew an arrow! Congratulations!

Now, if you want to get a little bit fancier, follow this formula to draw the perfect arrow every time:

EXERCISE

Draw picture-perfect arrow shapes

1. Start by drawing 3 sides of a rectangle.

2. Next, trace an imaginary line from the center of the short end of the container to where you want the point of the arrow to be.

3. Draw a dot a little way out from the middle of the container. Now put two dots on either side of the open end, equal distance apart.

4. Connect the dots to form a triangle and then attach it to the walls of the open container! Ta da! A fancy arrow you can color or write in or whatever you want!

If you play this kind of connect-the-dots arrow game, then you can use it to make all sorts of arrow shapes. You can make the body of the arrow as wild as you want to, and as long as you keep the point even at the end, it will look amazing.

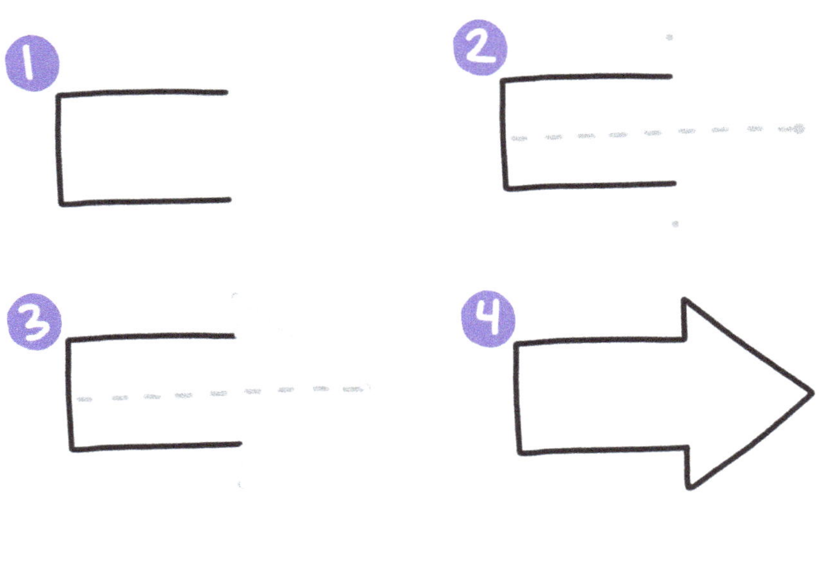

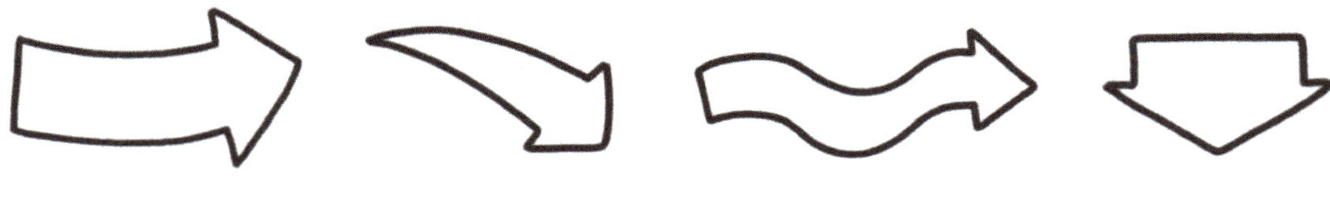

EXERCISE

Draw different arrow shapes

A variety of arrows and line styles will keep the drawing captivating while clearly showing the flow. Try a long arrow, a short and stubby arrow, a wavy arrow, and a zig zag. See the graphics at the end of this chapter for inspiration!

Scientists were finding that visual images were easier to remember than text as early as 1894! The phenomenon is known as the Picture Superiority Effect and has been demonstrated repeatedly using different methods over the past century.[6]

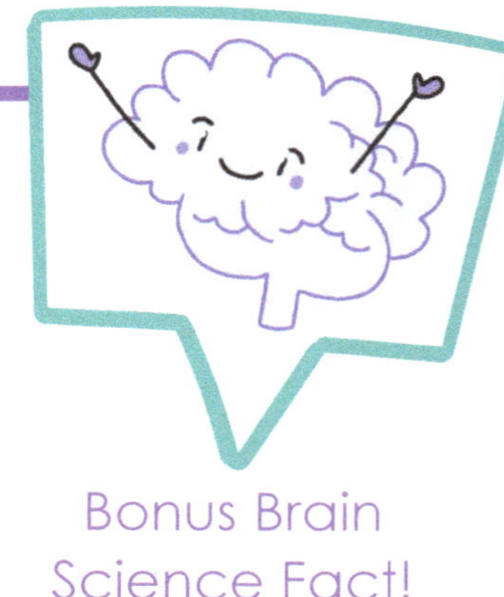

Bonus Brain
Science Fact!

Uses of Lines and Arrows

You can use lines and arrows to do the following things: show direction, build connections, and create separation.

Show Direction

If the presenter is moving smoothly from theme to theme, or if there's a clear development of ideas from start to finish, you can use lines and arrows to create a clear flow on the page. Then, when you return to your sketchnote to review it later, you'll be able to remember the sequence of information. The lines and arrows will guide you through the drawing and help you recall the path that you took.

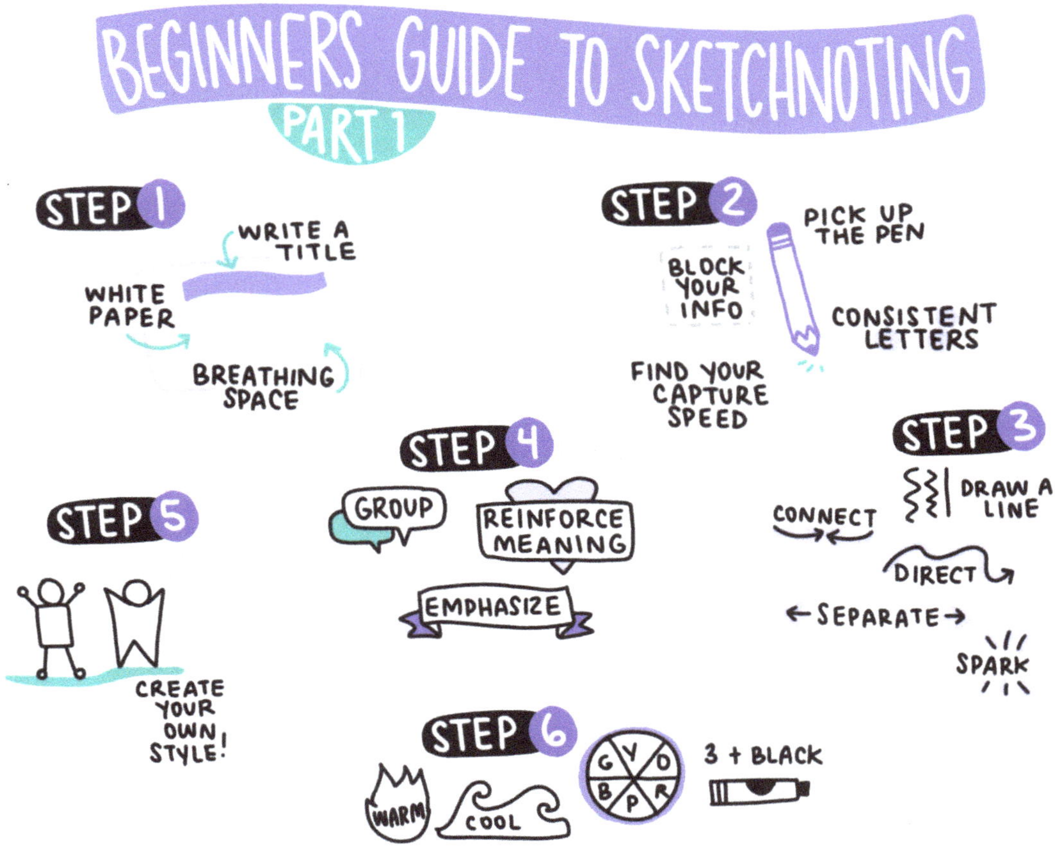

Build Connections

Sometimes the flow will branch off in different directions too, and that's ok! Conversations and information that's being shared aren't always linear, but as long as you're connecting themes effectively, you'll be able to read your sketchnote clearly.

Information might come up that's connected to a much earlier point, and that can be confusing without a visual cue. You can use lines and arrows to bridge concepts together and help yourself remember those connections.

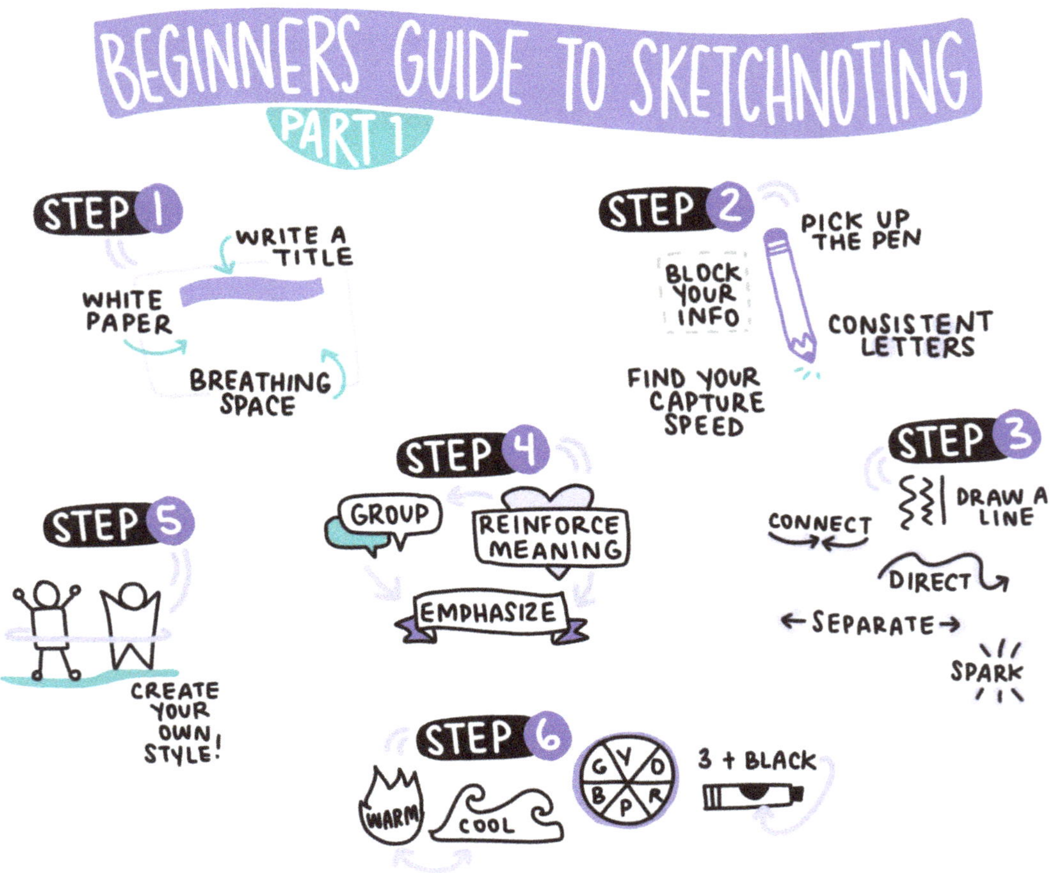

Create Separation

Sometimes we need to show what information is NOT connected! When this happens, we can use lines to show very strong separation in the sketchnote. It might be drawing small lines to separate smaller pieces of information or huge lines to completely divide out bigger sections of content.

You'll likely use more lines than arrows in this case, but feel free to play around with this concept!

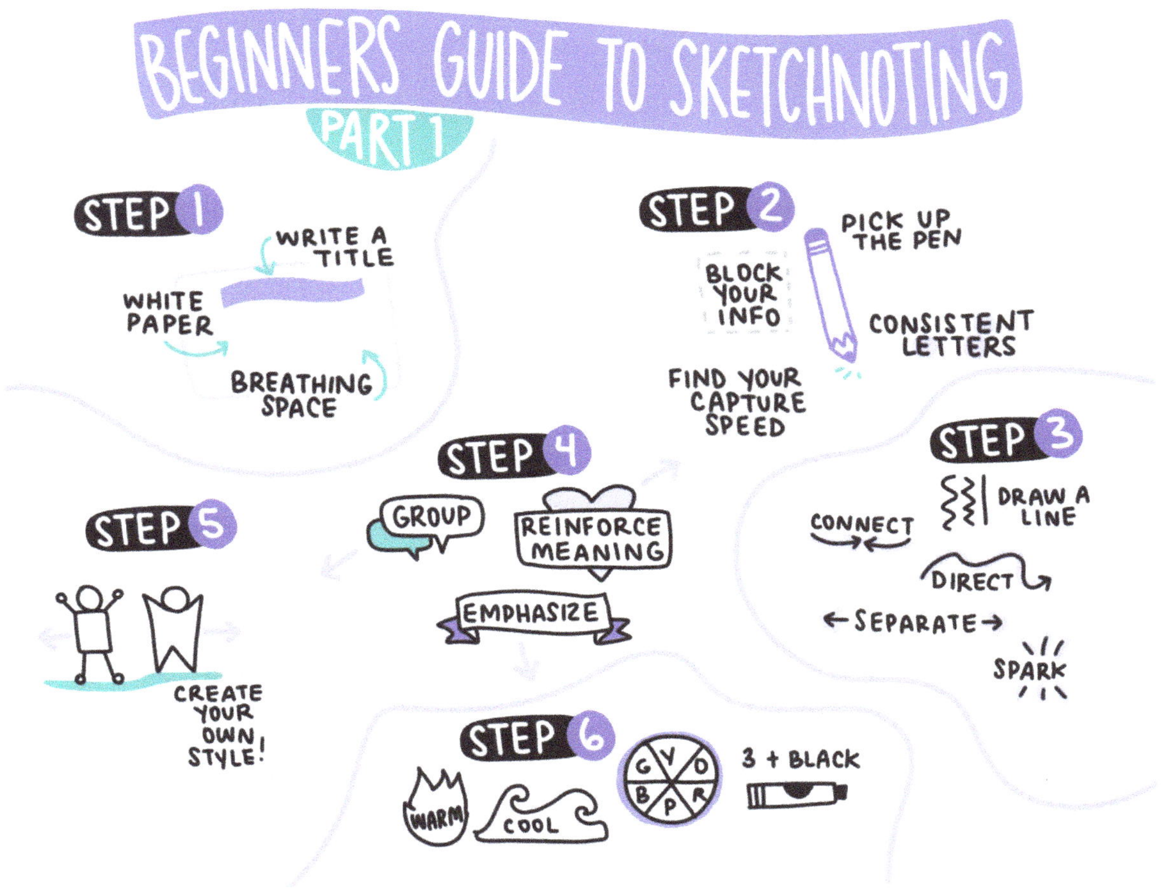

BEGINNERS GUIDE TO SKETCHNOTING
PART 1

Bonus: Spark Lines

If you want to highlight something or add some extra energy to your sketchnote, you can use spark lines. Spark lines are usually just small straight lines. Add them around graphics or words for extra emphasis.

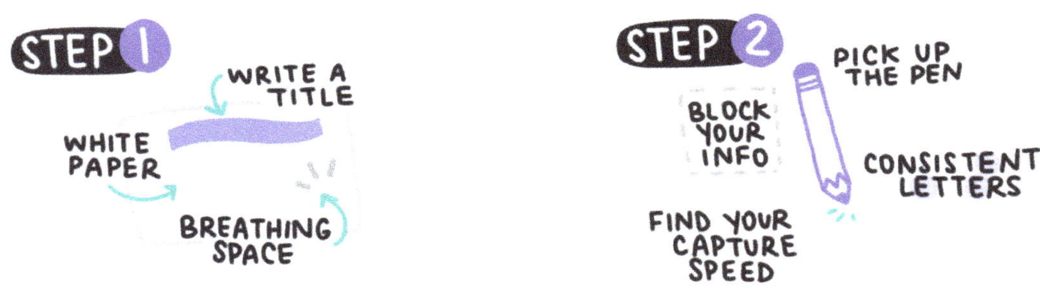

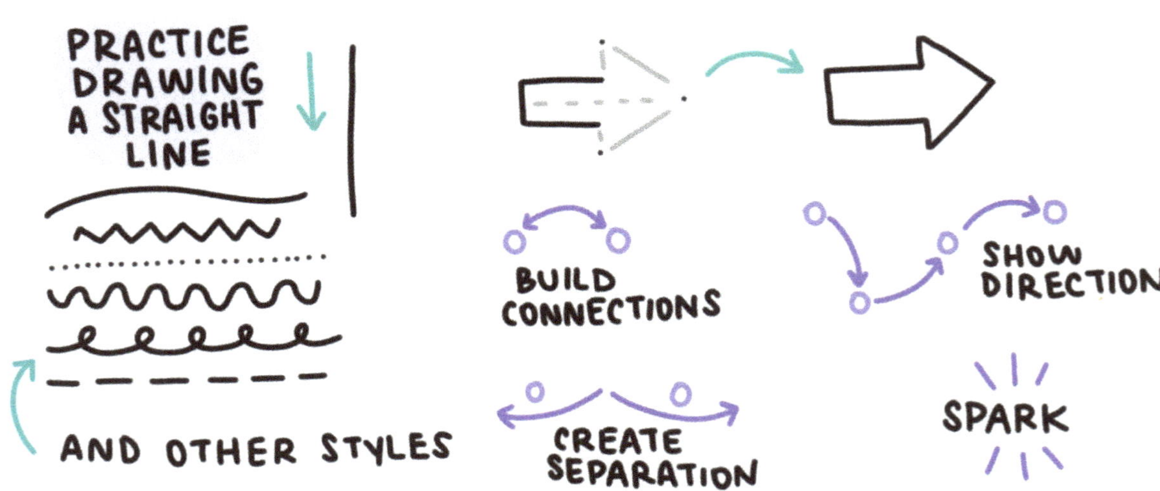

Here's my sketchnote about creating flow with lines and arrows. You can see how I used the elements of the chapter to highlight the words "lines" and "arrows" in the title. I drew out some examples of different lines and included the main lessons from the chapter, using the simple line drawings to express each idea. I also drew a condensed version of how to draw an arrow

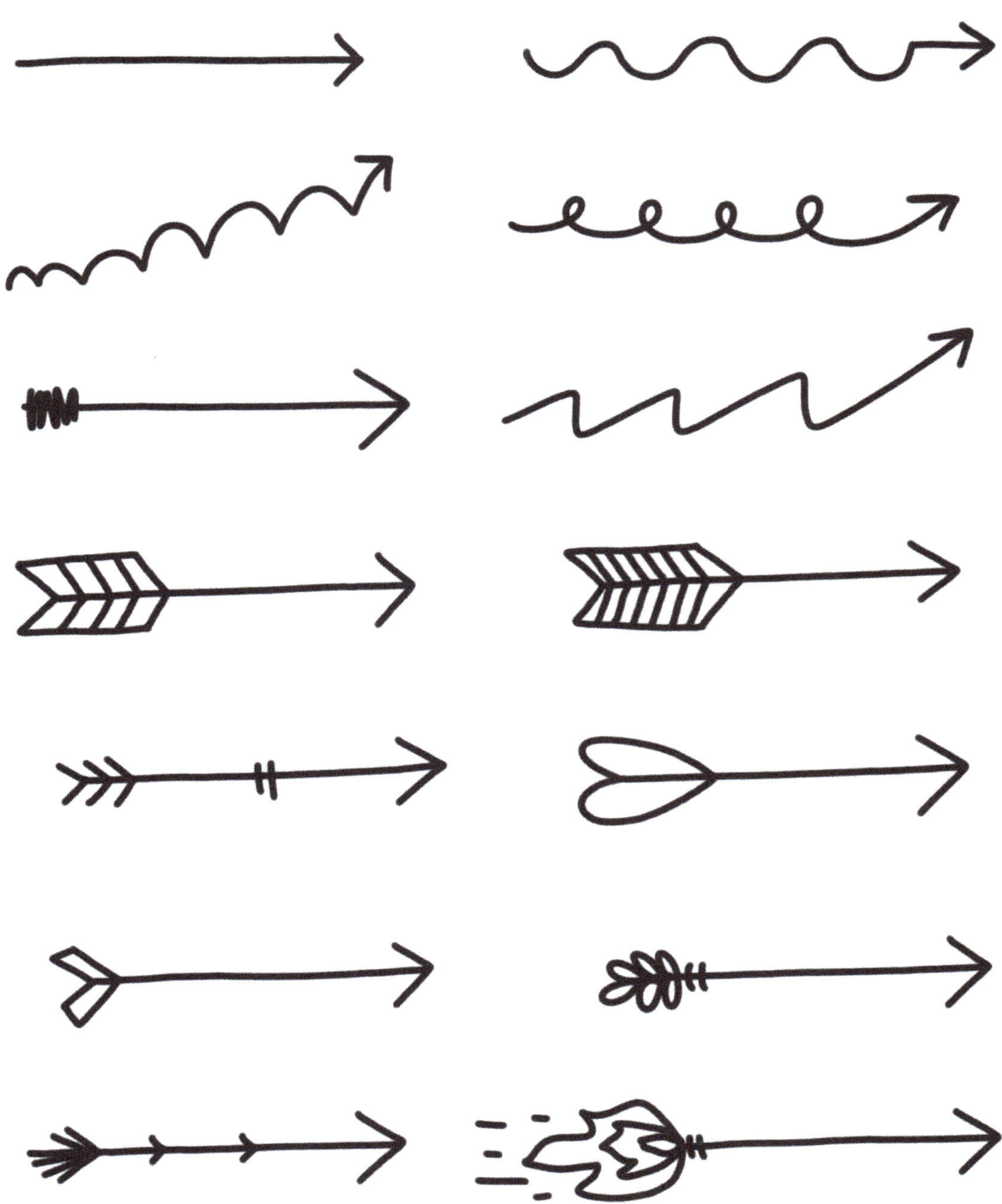

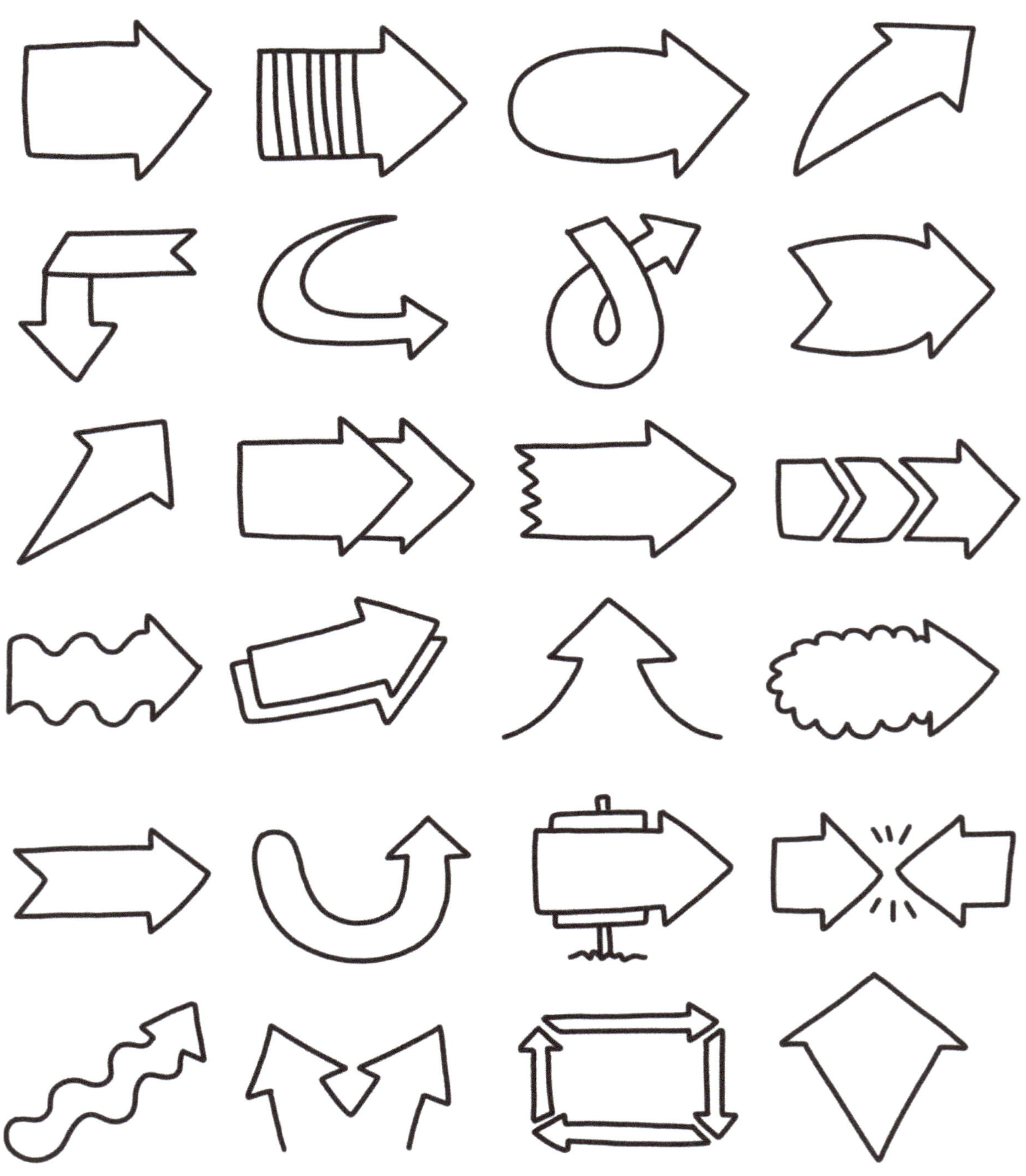

Cheat Sheet : Arrows

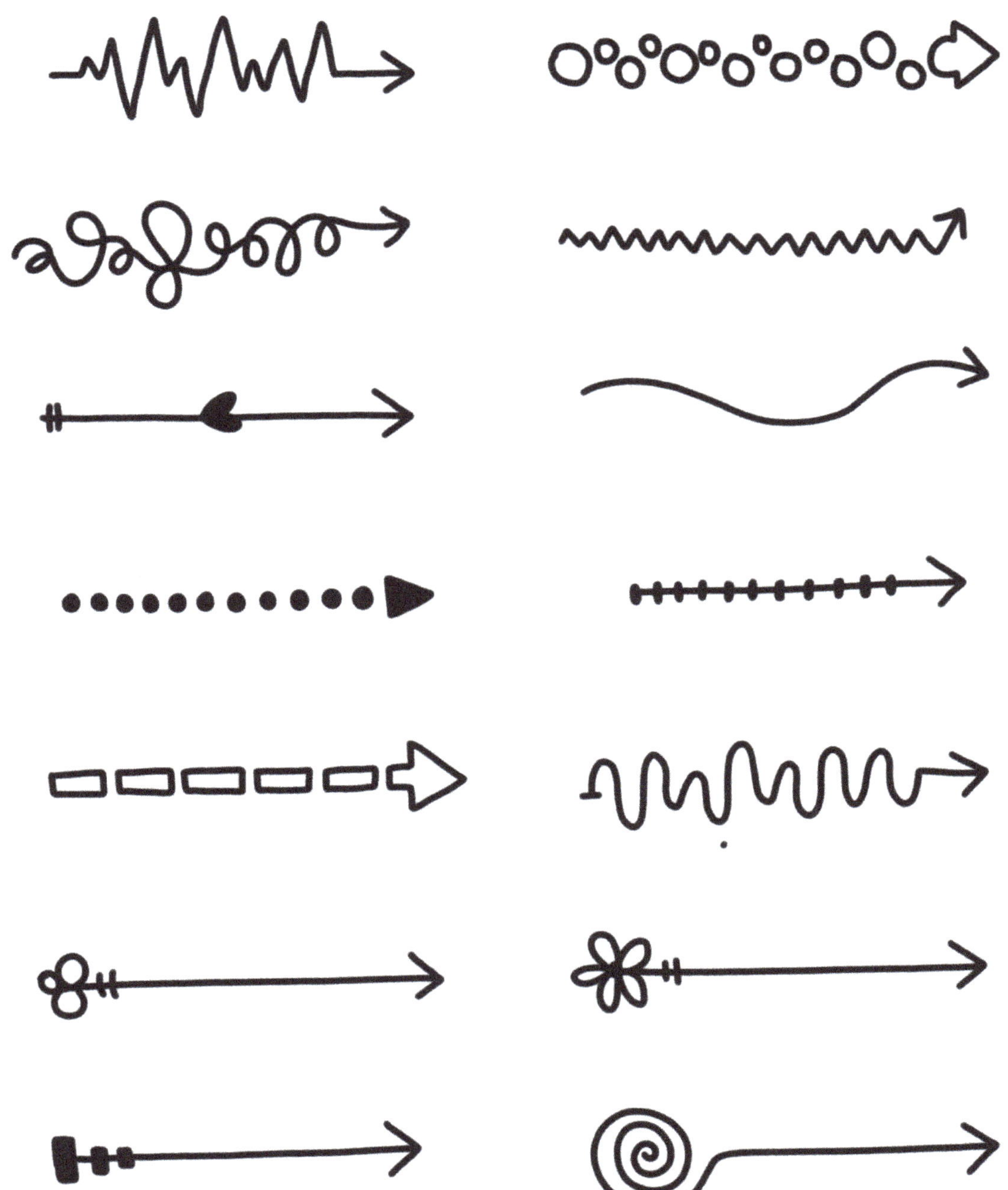

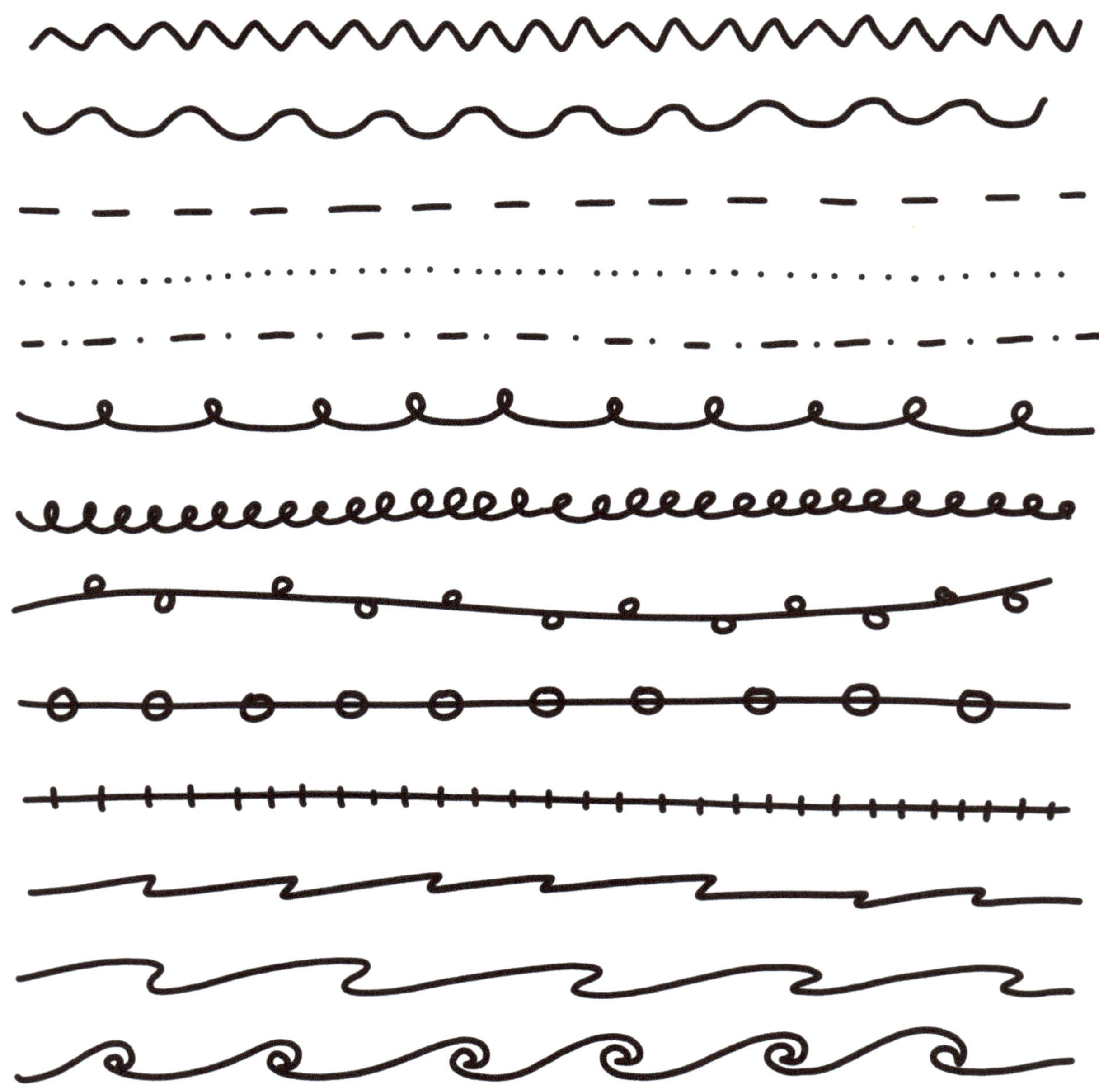

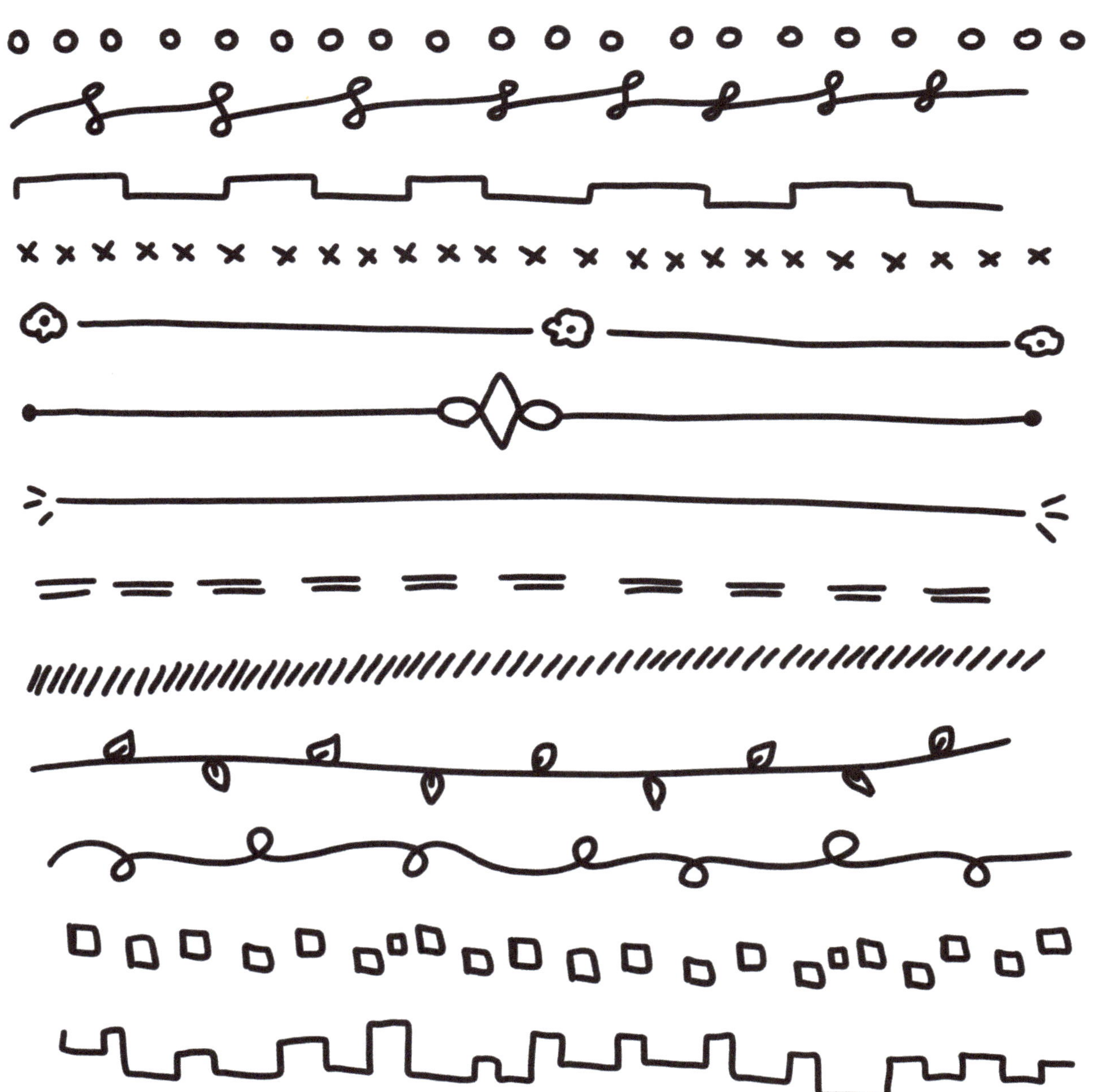

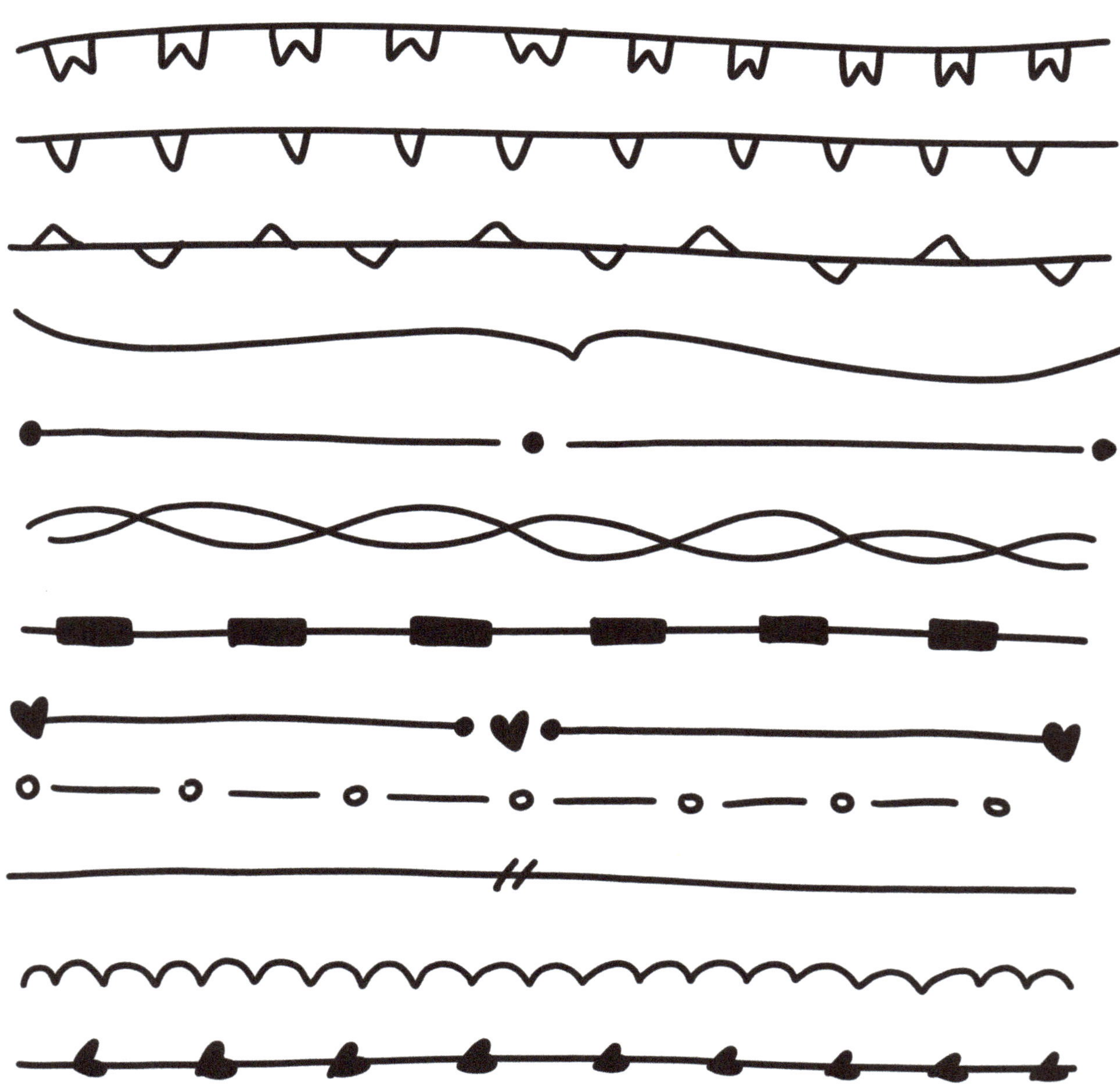

STEP 4 – ENHANCING CLARITY WITH CONTAINERS

Remember how we worked on blocking your content and writing in imaginary boxes? Well, a container is an actual box. It's any kind of shape or border that goes around information in your sketchnote.

Just like lines and arrows, containers can serve a few different purposes. They can help make your sketchnote clearer as well as bring it to life.

Let's look at some specific ways you can use containers:

Ways to Use Containers

You can use containers to do the following things: Group ideas, emphasize titles and subheadings, and reinforce meaning

Group Ideas

You can use containers to group ideas together. Containers are great if you have a lot of individual pieces of information but want to signify that they relate to one another.

You can make your containers the same shape, the same color, or both. You can also make them overlap each other to really emphasize the connections.

In this example, I've used containers to connect a group of related ideas. I've used matching colors in three of the examples and overlapping in two. As you can probably tell, my primary tactic for grouping ideas is using containers with similar shapes!

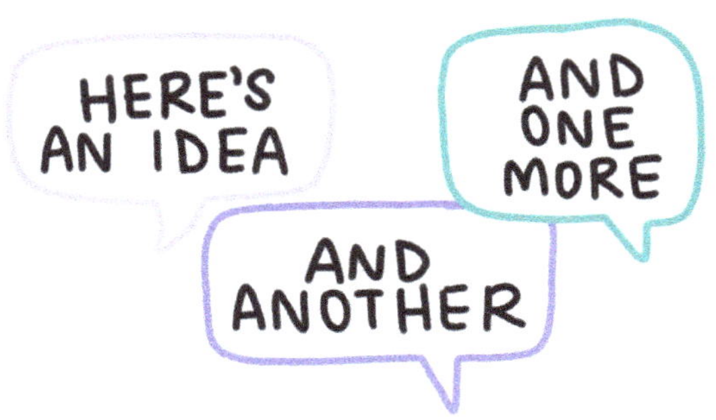

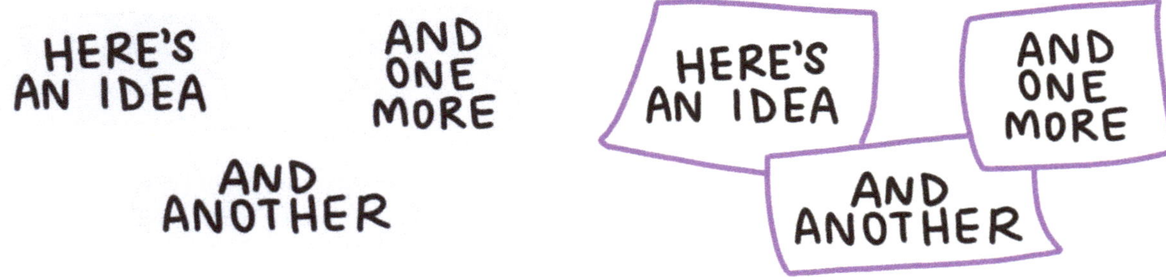

You can also group ideas together in one container. In the examples below you can see that only one (the last one) is completely enclosed in the container while the other two spill slightly outside the edges. This is a design choice.

You'll notice here that I'm using the "blocking content" method that we covered in Step 2. You can see how it's much easier to use containers around information when the information lives in these invisible blocks.

Important Note: Drawing too many containers can make them lose their meaning, so it's important not to overuse them.

While you're in the moment of sketchnoting, if you realize that information belongs together you can unify it more in a list format if you wish. This can help you later when you go to enclose it.

Emphasize Titles and Subheadings

Remember when we discussed different ways to communicate the hierarchy of information? Containers are great for this!

Using a container around important information makes it stand out from supporting details. Here we have a banner (a very popular style of container that's fun and easy to draw—see the end of the chapter for a step-by-step guide). I used the banner to contain a subject heading, and then wrote some supporting ideas underneath it.

This is a practical and visually appealing way to highlight the main theme.

Bonus: I used some bullets of the same style and color too, to showcase that the different points also belong here.

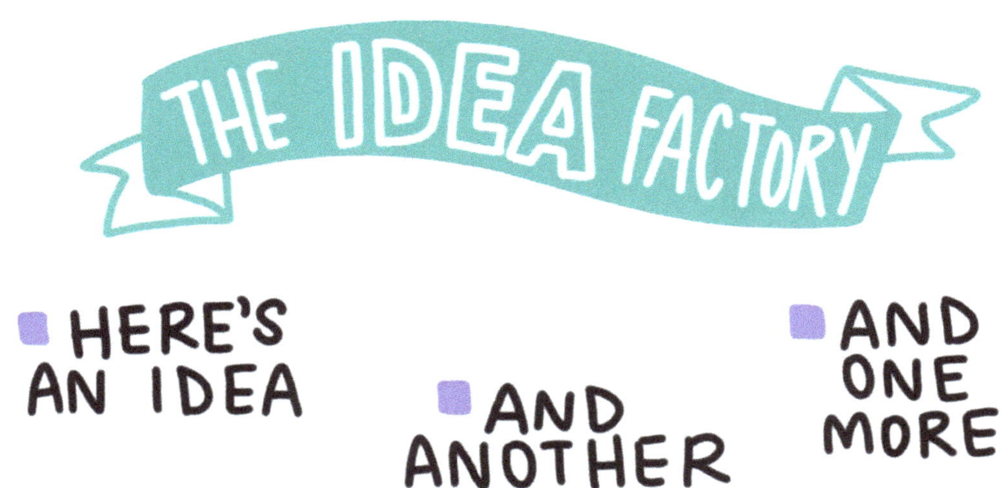

Reinforce Meaning

You can also use containers as embellishments that reinforce the meaning of the information while bringing your page to life visually.

Using containers this way is a very intuitive process, and you can make it as simple or complicated as you're comfortable with. Whatever feels right in the moment is perfect!

Here are some examples that you can try right away. Don't feel like you have to limit yourself to these, though. This is a fantastic way to start adding more "drawing" elements that connect to the meaning of the information. The more comfortable you get, the more fun you can have! Using containers in this way is starting to build your visual vocabulary which we'll talk more about in part two of the book.

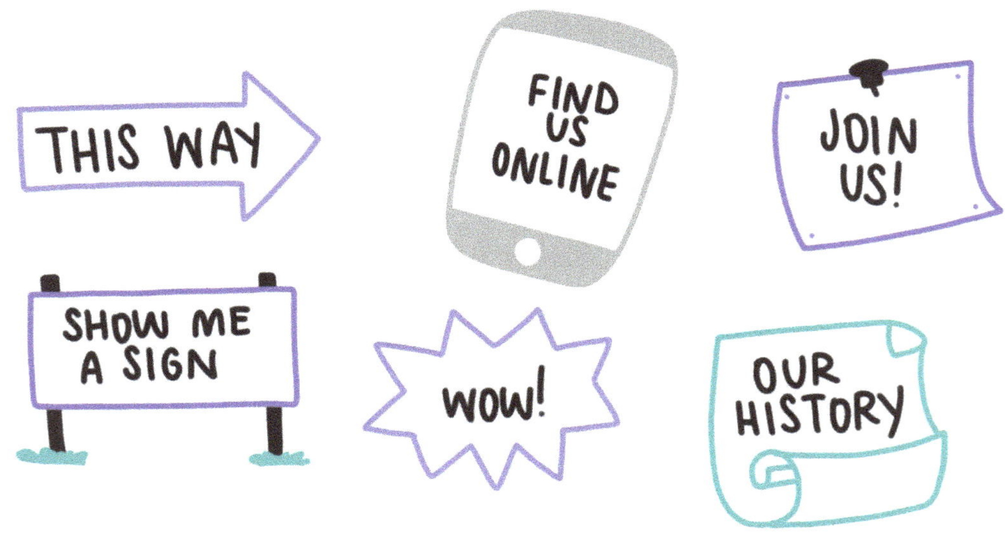

Get Playful With it!

On the following page is an example of expressing one idea in six different ways using the same computer container. Once you know how to draw the computer shape, change it up slightly.

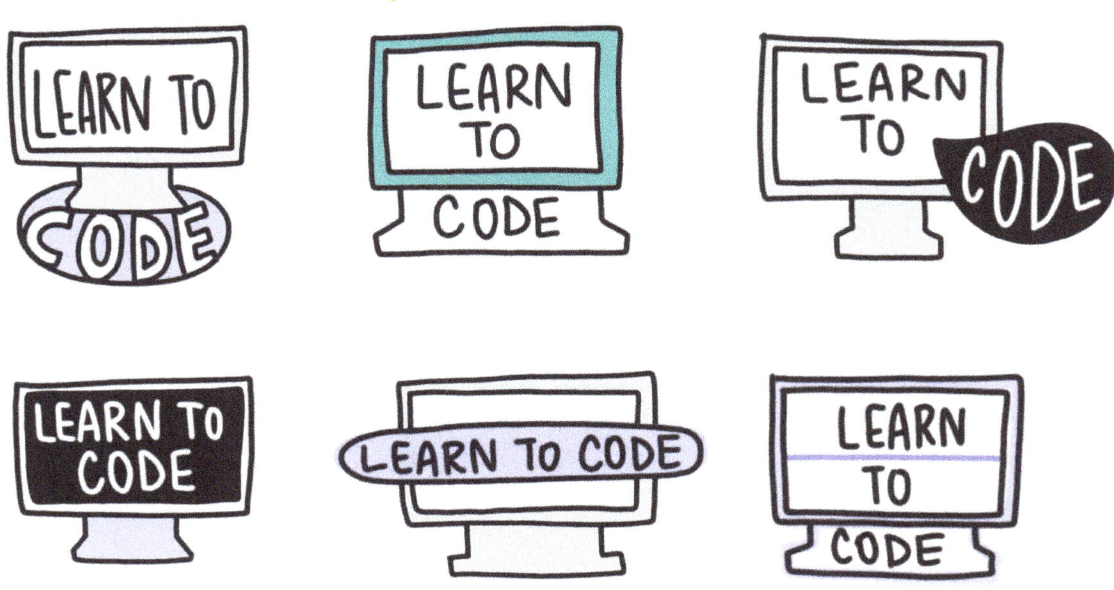

Bonus: You'll notice that I used white lettering on a black background in a couple of these examples. You can do this on any dark background to add some extra visual interest and make the words stand out. It's easier to do it digitally, but you can make it work on paper too!

Wait to Draw Your Container

Don't worry about putting containers around things right away. Always capture the information first. Just make sure you leave enough space to draw containers around your content blocks.

Waiting to contain the information keeps you safe from the horrible feeling of realizing your text won't fit in a box you've pre-drawn. I'm convinced that EVERYONE has done this at least once.

Containing your information when you're finishing up your sketchnote also means that if any related information comes up later, you can add it where it belongs without worrying about space. Once you have an idea of the content, you'll be able to tell where containers need to go and what shape or design would be most effective. Once you build up your muscle memory you can cheat this a little bit since you'll have a better sense of your space.

When Should You Use a Line or Arrow and When Should You Use a Container?

This is a bit like the question, "Which came first, the chicken or the egg?"—it's impossible to answer!

All you really have to do is trust your instincts. There will be more times when it makes more sense to use containers and other times when you'll feel like arrows will work better. The key is to start incorporating them all when you're ready. That's when things get fun and your sketchnote starts to come together.

Play around with all three elements (lines, arrows, and containers) at the same time. Make decisions in the moment. After you're done with one sketchnote (and without being too hard on yourself) ask yourself what you could have changed to better show the flow and contain the information more clearly.

What worked? What didn't?
What did you like?
What would you like to try on the next sketchnote you do?

EXERCISE

Experiment with creative containers

Did you know that containers don't have to be simple squares or rectangles? Not only can containers be any shape you want, but you can easily turn them into more detailed drawings as well! For example, I can turn a square-ish container into a notepad, a poster, and a clipboard with just a few additional lines.

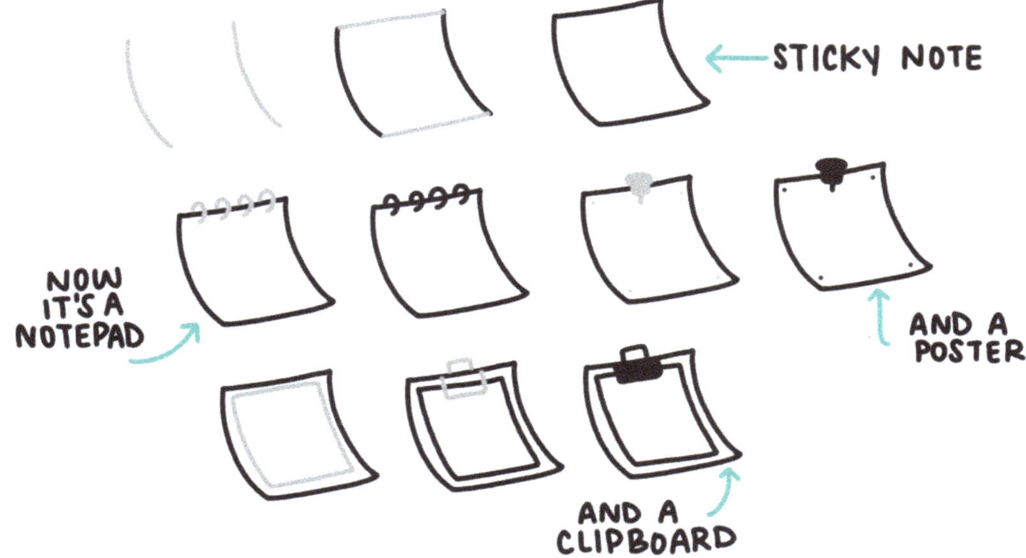

Play around with shapes and see what you like best.

As you can see we are starting to add more elements of "drawings" into your sketchnote and starting to build your visual vocabulary, which we will dive into more in the second part of the book.

EXERCISE

Container practice

Draw 10 shapes you could use to contain information in your sketchnotes. Plan to add one or two of them to your example sketchnote as you continue through this book!

If you're stumped, head to the end of this chapter for a cheat sheet of ideas.

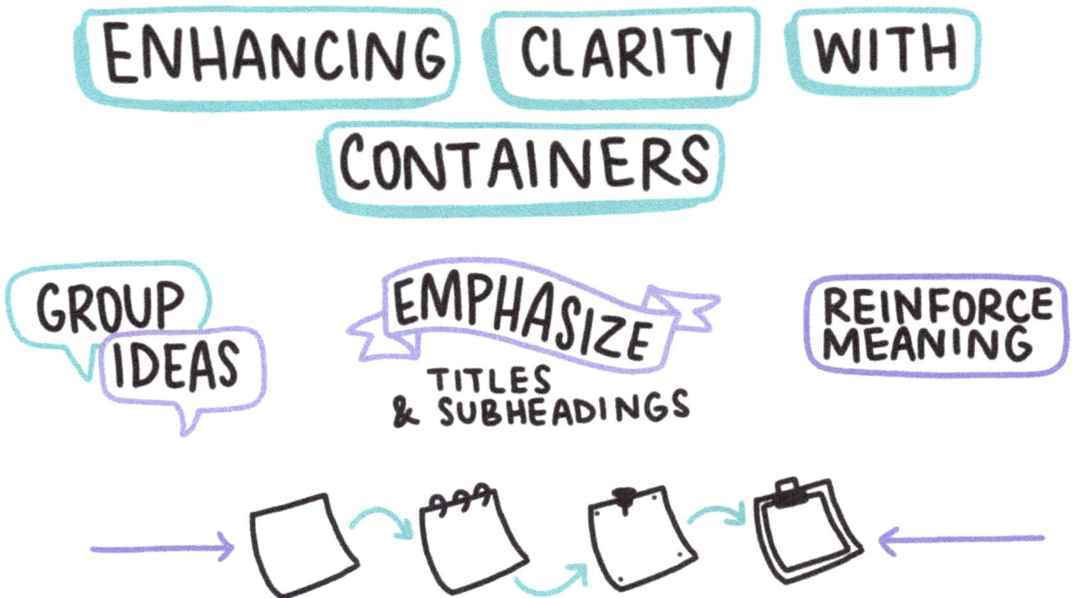

For this summary sketchnote, I decided to be a bit cheeky with the title and put containers around each word (just another example of using themes in your titles). I pulled out the three main lessons from the chapter and summarized them simply using different containers. Then I drew out a condensed version of the square and how you can make it into other shapes.

Cheat Sheet : Containers

Cheat Sheet : Drawing a Banner

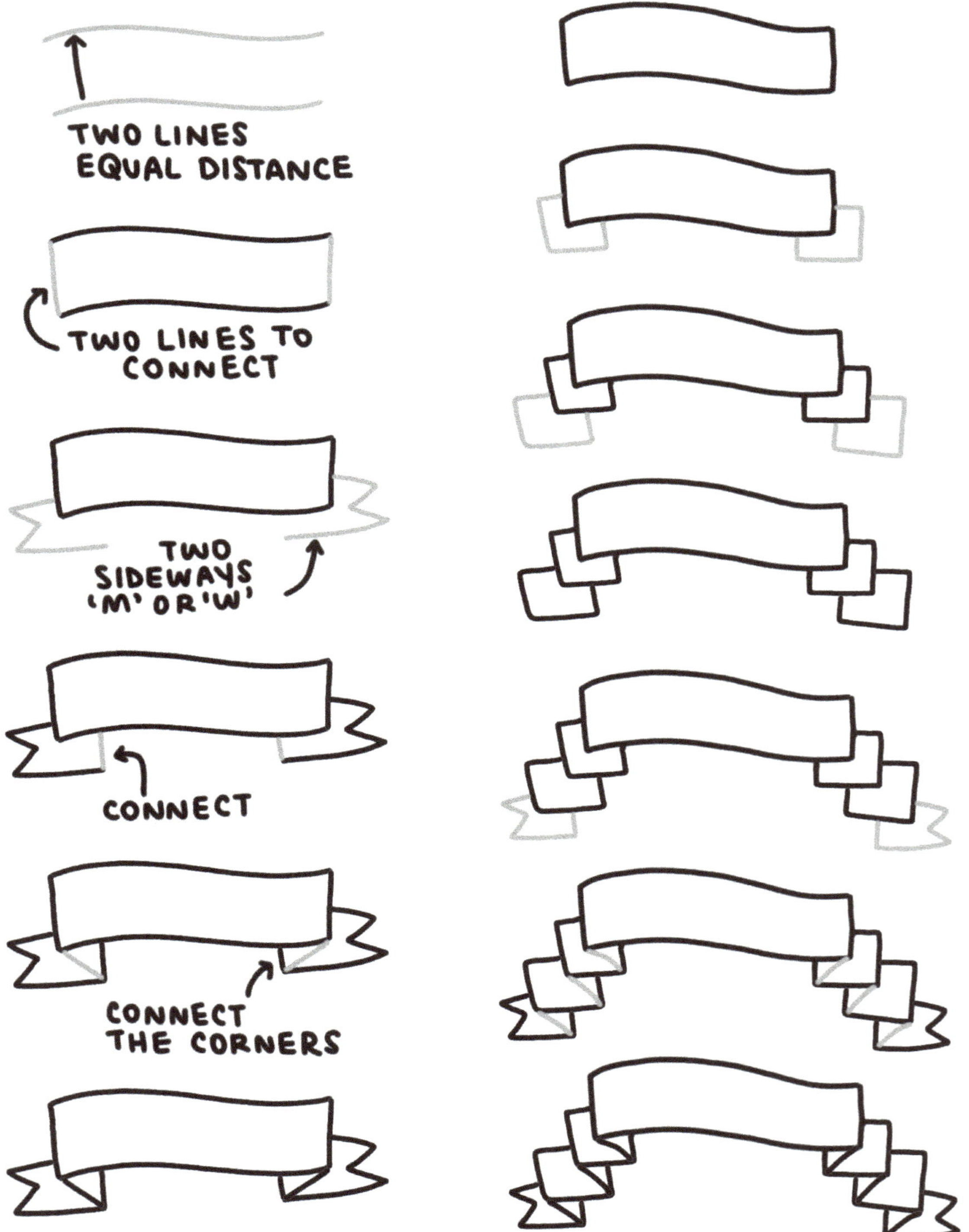

STEP 5 – DRAWING PEOPLE IS EASY

Drawing people or faces in your sketchnotes can help humanize the information you're capturing. You can draw faces or figures to represent people who are quoted or come up in the discussion. They're a nice stepping stone in your sketchnoting process.

But here's the thing: the people you draw don't have to be complicated or lifelike! They just need to be recognizable as people. In fact, when someone tells me they can only draw stick figures, my immediate response is, "Great! Let's get started!"

You Can Draw People!

You've already had practice drawing lines, boxes, and circles. And drawing a person is as easy as combining these elements!

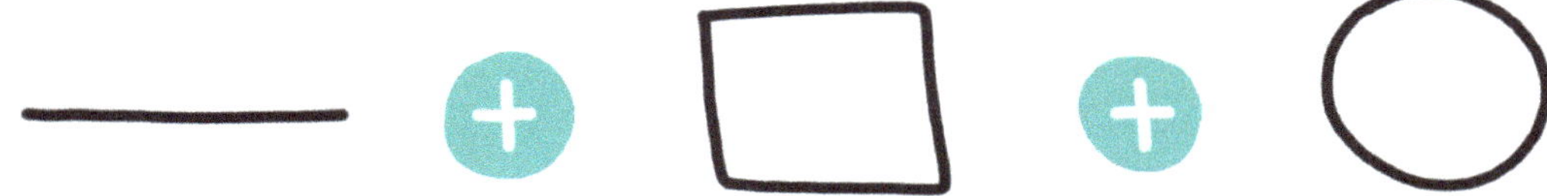

Draw a rectangle, then four lines—one from each corner. Draw a circle at the top of the rectangle, plus small circles at the end of each line. Ta-da! A person! Told you it was easy!

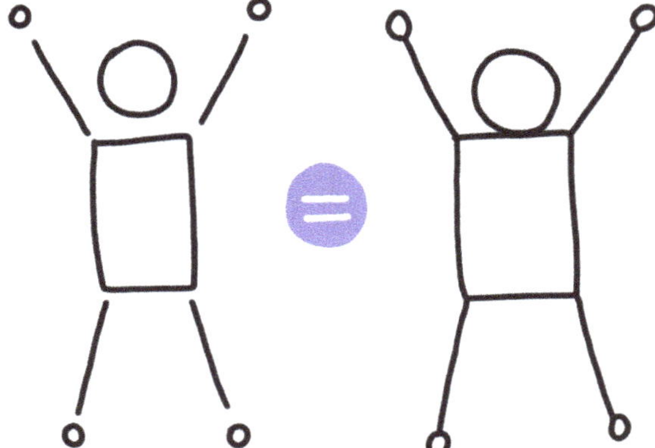

Another sweet, simple way of drawing people is called a star person. The top point of the star becomes a circle for the head. You can then move the arms and legs around in different directions to show your person doing different things. I love star people because they're easy to draw, and they're also adorable!

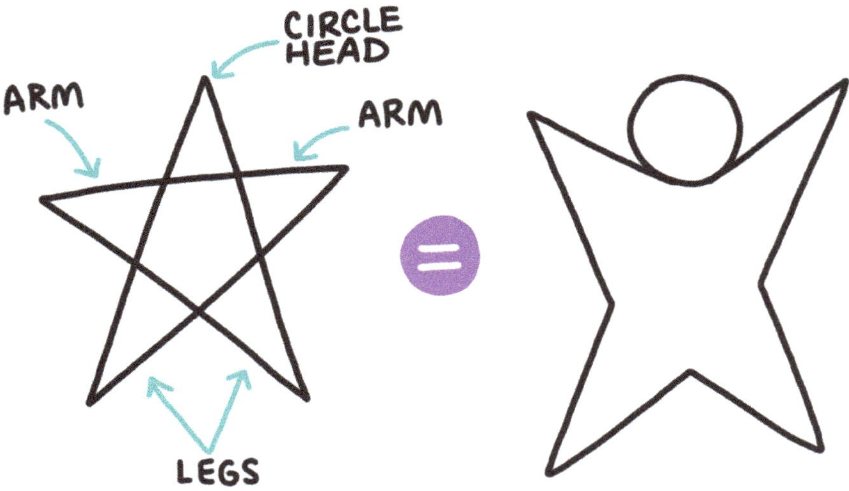

There are no limits to the kinds of people you can draw! Here are a few more ideas to play with—but don't feel like you have to stick to these!

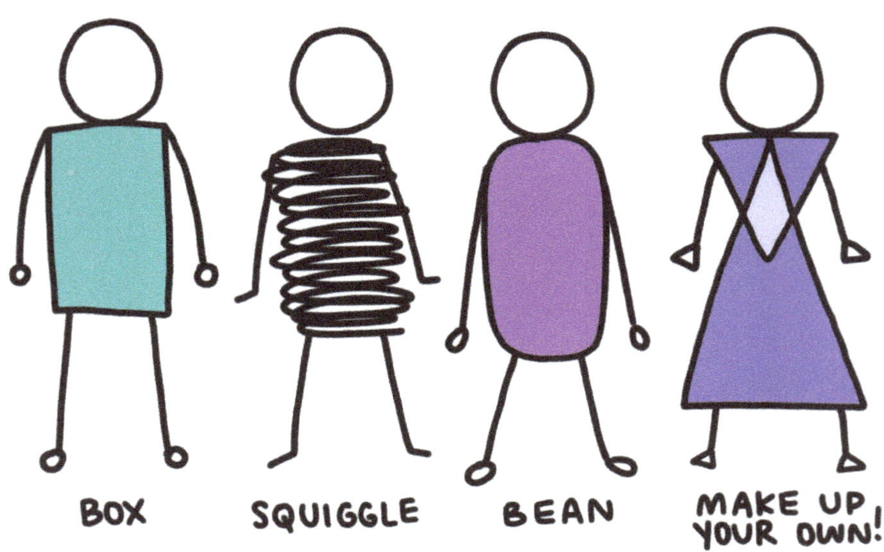

Once you have the basic shape down, you can make your people do all kinds of things! Move the arms and legs around to make different shapes and actions. Body language is a powerful communication tool and you'll find that your little figures can say a lot even without faces!

You don't have to be a trained artist or include lots of detail in order for a sketchnote to be effective! As Wendi Pillars shares in her book *Visual Note-taking for Educators*, "Sometimes the simpler the drawing the better—a drawing only needs to represent 30% of reality for us to recognize it."[7]

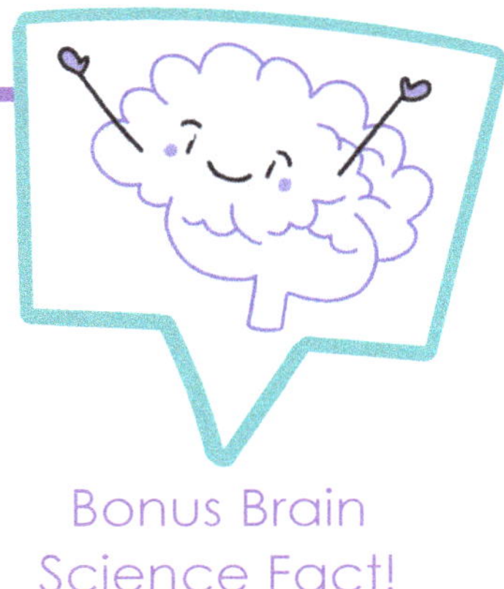

Bonus Brain Science Fact!

Feel Free to Draw Just a Face!

Should you draw just the face or the whole body? This is part personal preference, part timing. If you're drawing a star or box person, then drawing the body is pretty simple, but if you're drawing more complex and detailed people then you'll need to manage how much time you have.

Ask yourself whether the face or the body specifically helps to reinforce the point you're capturing. If you feel like a body isn't going to add value to your topic then you could leave it out. That being said, if you're capturing a presentation about body positivity, for example, then drawing bodies of all shapes and sizes would be important. Consider your context!

Fill in the faces

Let's make some faces. Here's a few for inspiration:

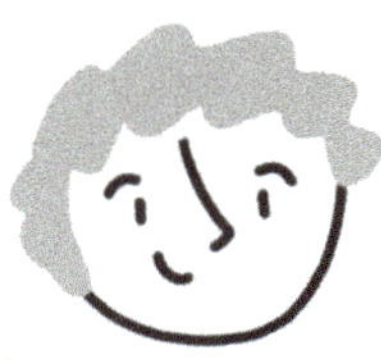 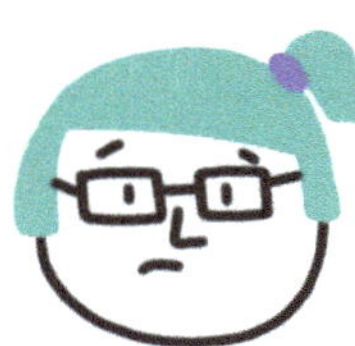 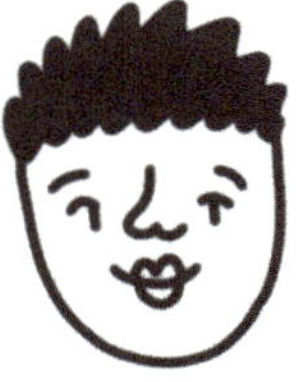  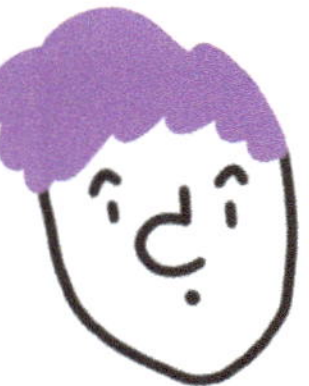

Here are some faces with just the eyebrows. What emotions do you think the person is feeling based on their eyebrows? Fill in the rest of the face!

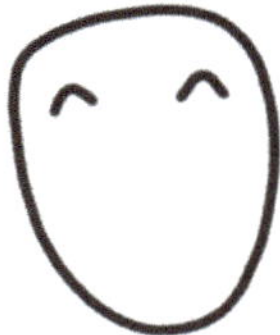 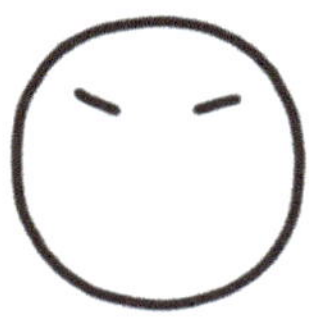 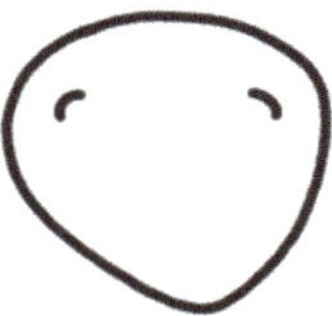 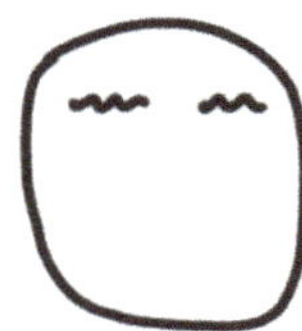 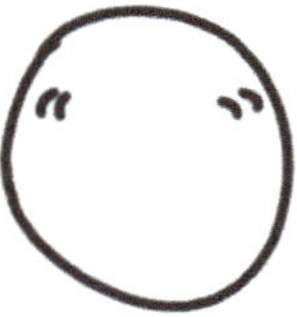

Now, how about just the mouth? What do you think this person is feeling? Fill in the rest of the face!

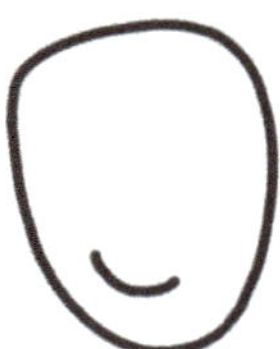 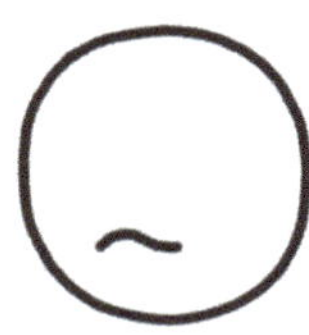 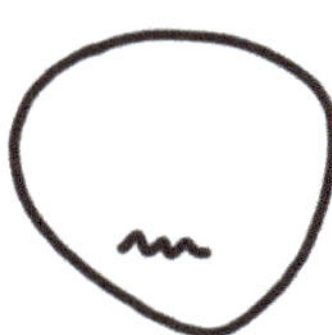 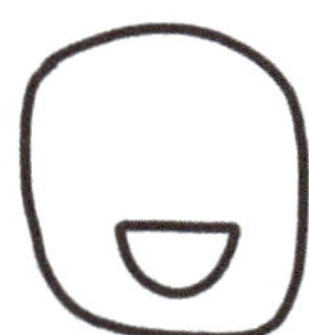 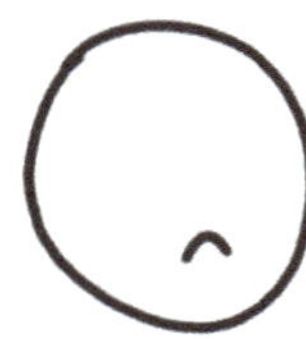

Now try your own! Play around with different shaped noses and eyes too! Don't forget to add some hair!

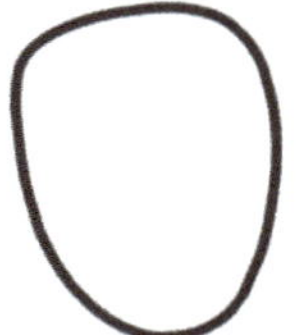 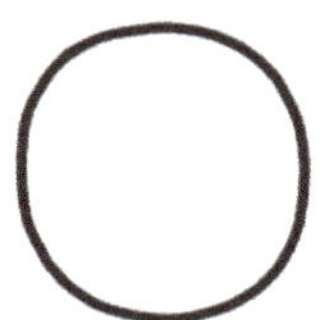 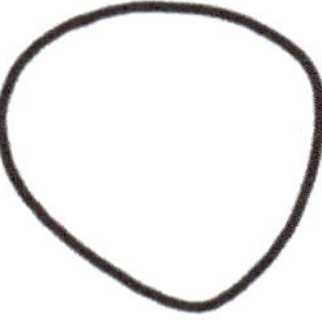 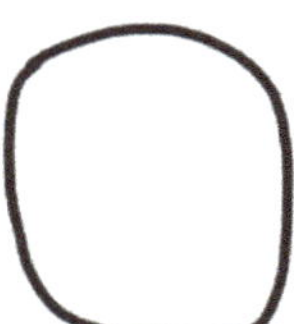 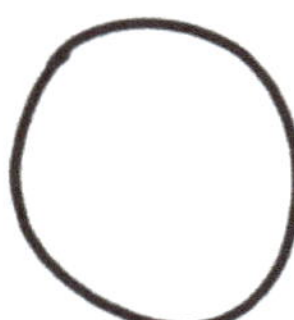

Draw Diverse Faces

You can add diversity to your sketchnote by drawing people with different features. For example, I sometimes will add a mole on someone's face, draw a person wearing a hijab, or have them wearing glasses. You can also change the face shape, nose, eyes, and hair.

I often start out by drawing a simple smiley face and then start adding element after element to see what I like best. Play around with this but please avoid stereotypes or things that may be culturally inappropriate.

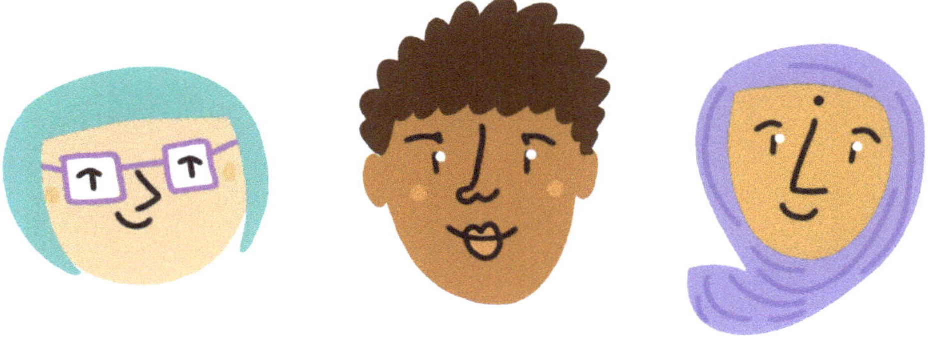

If you're not sure what to draw, using different face shapes can be a really simple starting point for showing diversity. The faces in the example above have a variety of shapes—and here are a few more examples:

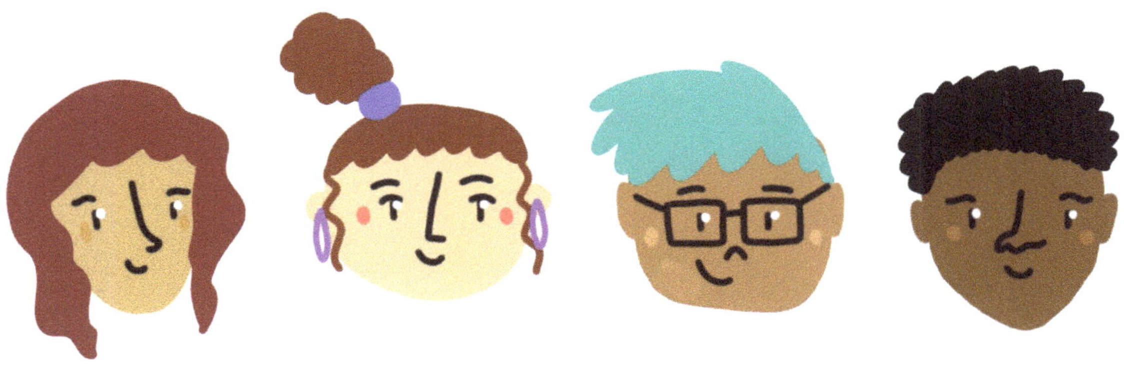

Draw a self portrait

Look at a photo of yourself in the mirror or pull up the selfie view on your phone. Look at your main features and things that make you uniquely you. Are you wearing earrings? Is your hair straight or curly? Do you wear glasses or have a scar in your eyebrow like I do?

Try drawing your own self portrait. Keep it simple and use basic lines and circles. Remember it's just for fun (and practice)!

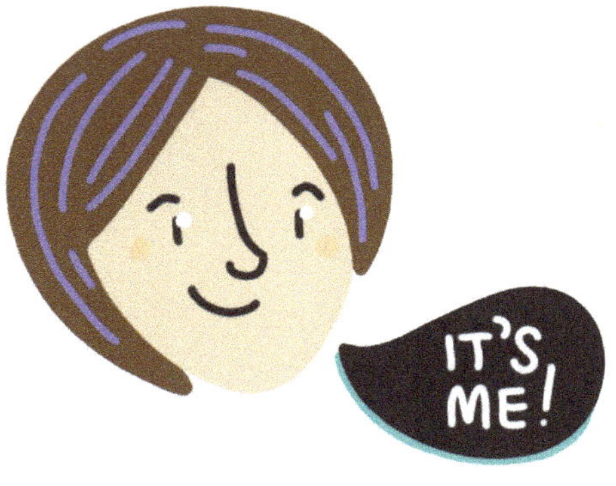

An Anecdote About Creating Your Own Style

When I began my journey in sketchnoting, I really had to warm up to the idea of drawing people.

I decided to go back to how I used to draw people when I was younger. Though I didn't actually draw a lot back then, I did have a certain way I drew people. For my first 2 or so years of sketchnoting, I would draw a combination of these people as well as star people. I wasn't loving it though, so I decided to change it up a bit.

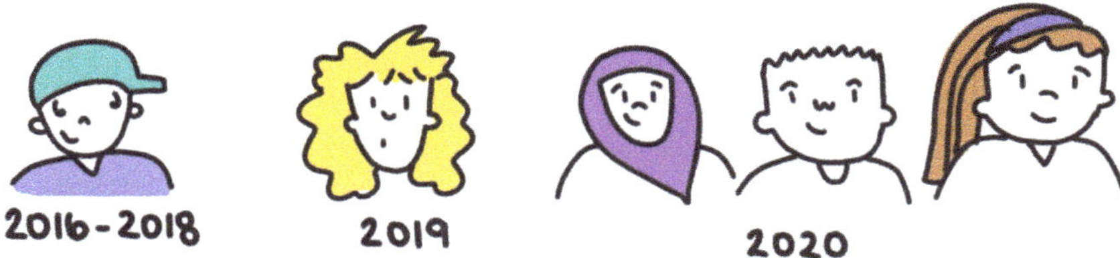

I first decided to change the way I drew eyes and started drawing people with just little lines for eyes. I would practice over and over again on large pieces of paper on the wall, drawing these people's faces as fast as I possibly could.

Then I decided I wanted to make the people a bit more diverse, so I started playing around with hair and nose shapes.

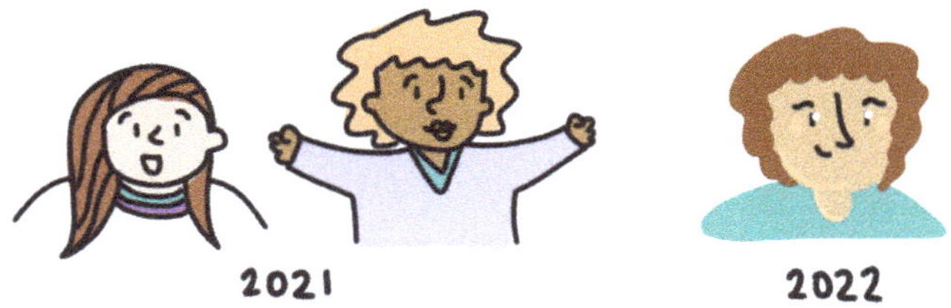

I love black and often draw everything in black first, so early on I would outline the faces in black and then fill them in with whatever skin tone I was using. Then in 2021/2022 I started to skip the black outline on faces and do a simple outline in the skin color instead.

Your style is going to change and morph over time. As you can see, I didn't force my style to happen. It was an organic process that happened over a period of years. Next year my people might even change again, who knows!

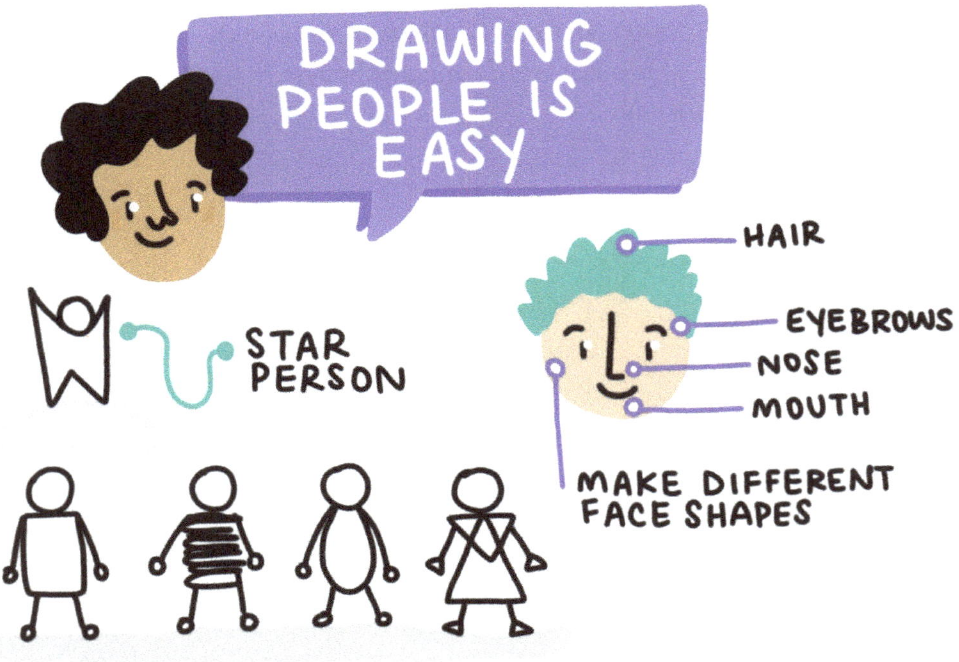

In this sketchnote you'll see that I included the different kinds of people as a reminder of how many simple options there are. I also chose to draw out the different elements of a face. I kept it pretty basic with these friendly reminders as a summary of this chapter.

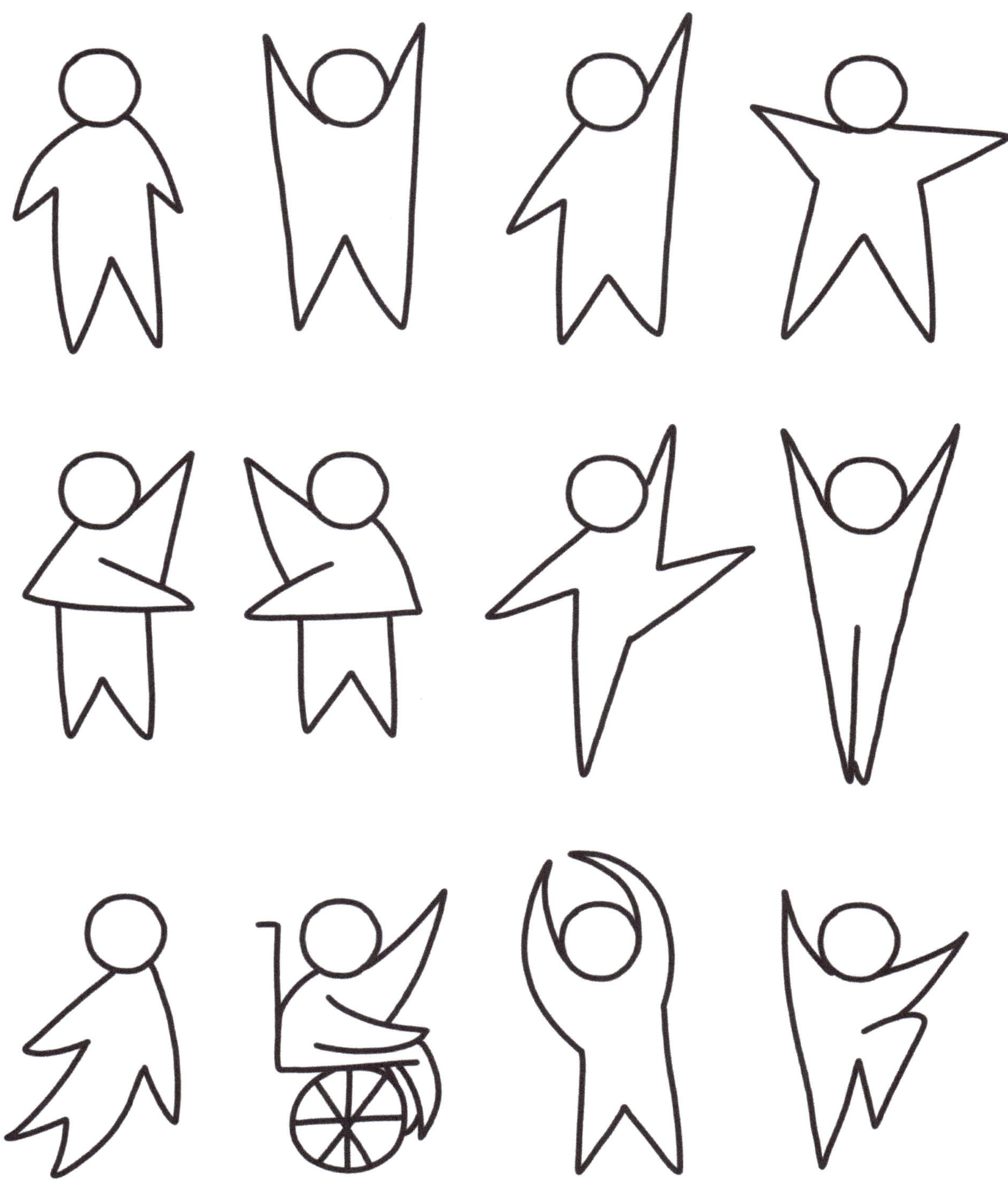

Cheat Sheet : Bean People

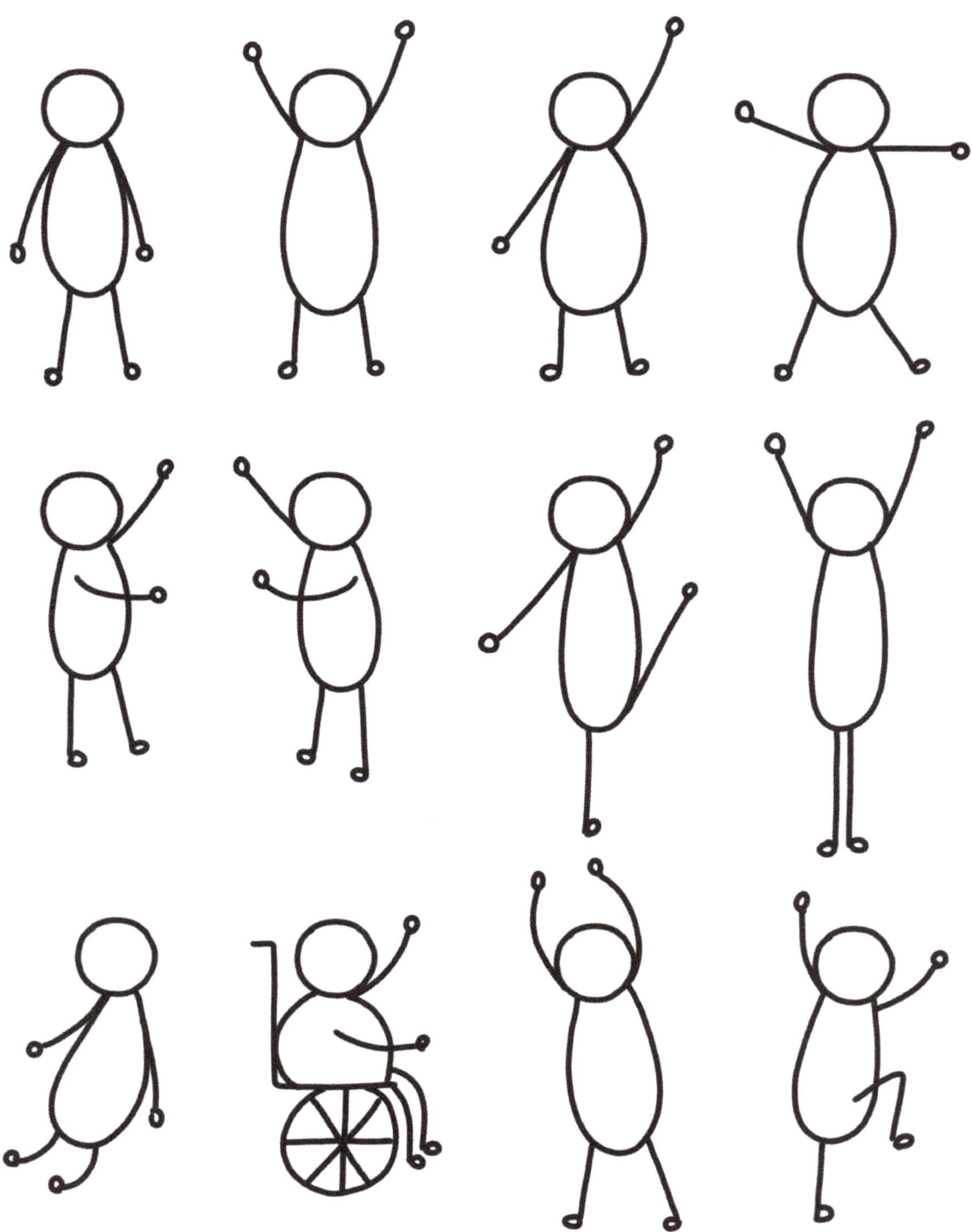

Cheat Sheet : Box People

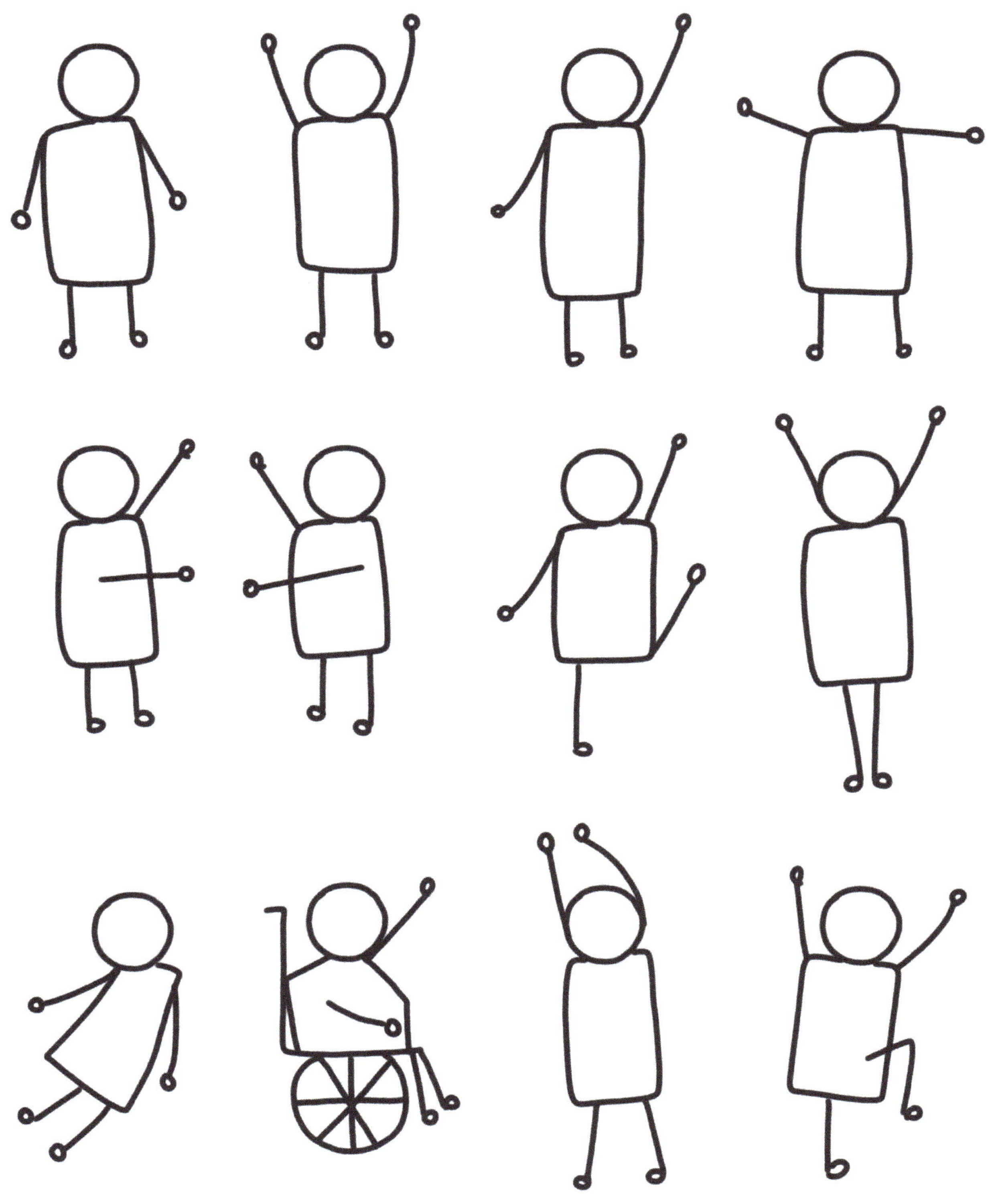

Cheat Sheet : Squiggle People

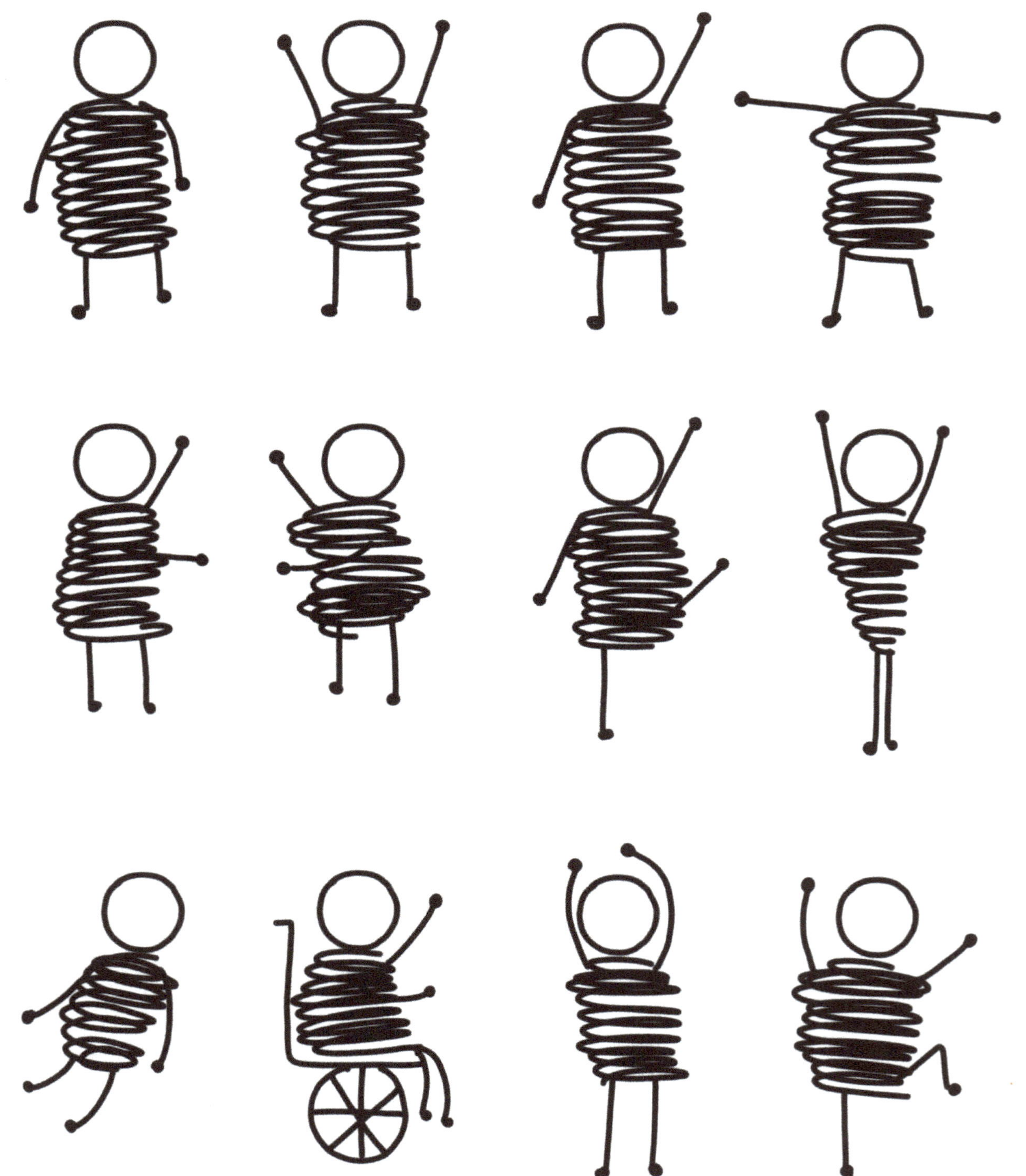

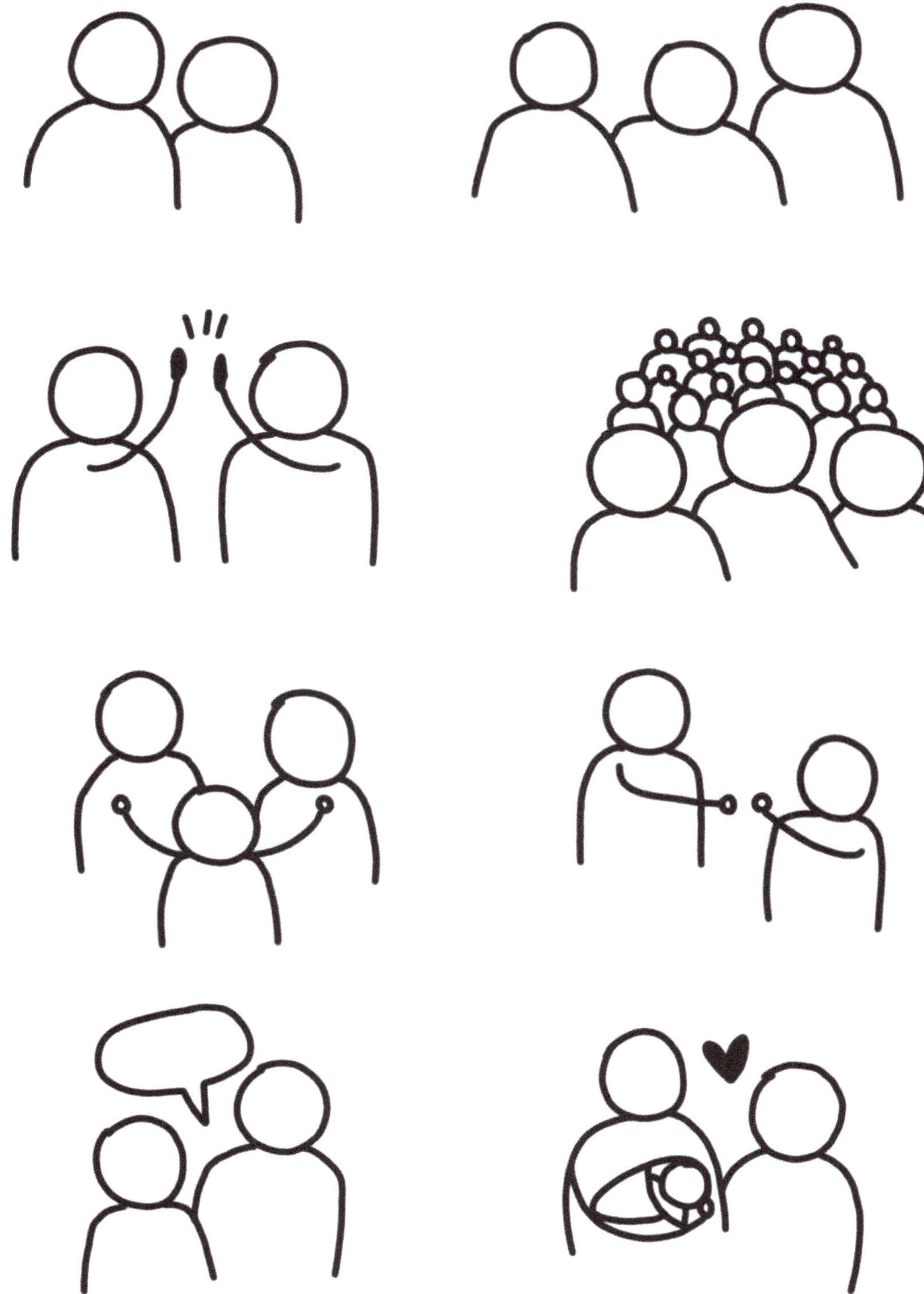

STEP 6 – ADDING PIZZAZZ WITH COLOR

You can create amazing, meaningful sketchnotes using nothing but a pencil or a pen—with no additional color at all!

BUT if you want to create something a bit more eye-catching, you can bring some color into the mix! Keep it simple and don't let yourself get overwhelmed!

Here's some basic color theory to get you thinking:

Explore Warm and Cool Colors

Warm colors are red, yellow, and orange. These colors make us feel warm and make us think of things like fire.

Cool colors are blue, green, and purple. These colors make us feel cool and make us think of things like the ocean.

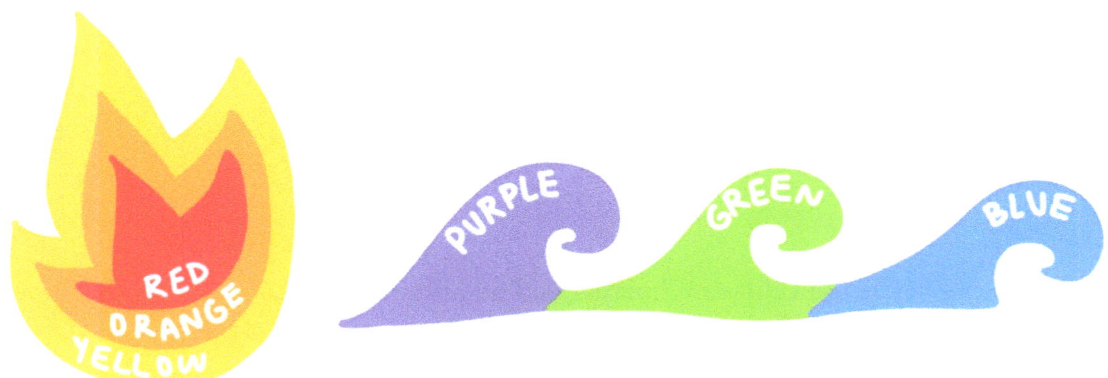

Play With the Color Wheel

Art students everywhere learn color theory based on the color wheel. It's basically a wheel that shows the relationship between colors. Common color choices are either analogous (two or three colors that are next to each other on the wheel—red, orange, and yellow are perfect examples) or complementary (2 colors from opposite sides of the wheel).

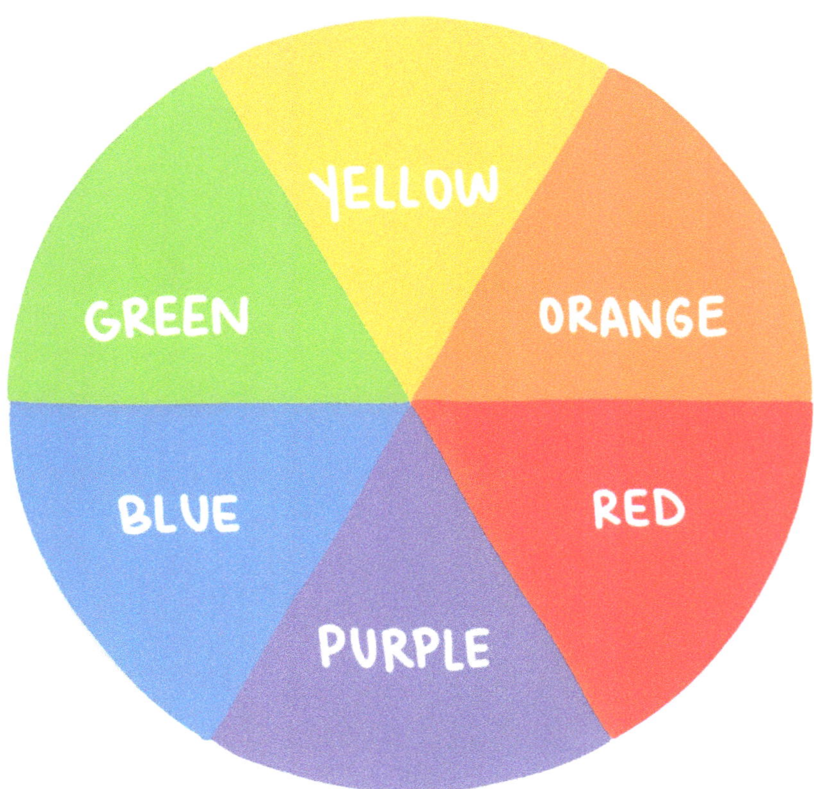

Complementary colors are yellow and purple, red and green, and blue and orange. These pairs create that "wow" factor when they're used together. They can really make your drawing come to life.

Think about sports teams—many of them use complementary colors to make their uniforms stand out. My favorite example is the LA Lakers: their purple and yellow jerseys are eye-catching and make their players easy to spot on the court!

How Many Colors to Use

A general rule, that I learned from Brandy Agerbeck, is three colors + black (or whatever your main lettering color happens to be).[8] Using a limited palette like this makes it easy for me to hold all the markers I'll be using in one hand while I draw with the other.

Deciding your colors before you begin can help you stay focused on the information instead of digging in your bag for another color or making those decisions on the fly when you need to focus on listening.

Remember: color is optional and a personal choice! Do what feels good for you!

That being said, it's important to consider visual accessibility if you're planning on sharing your notes with others. As a general rule of accessibility, stick with high contrast colors (using light colors on dark and dark colors on light). There are lots of tools available for color accessibility. You'll find more about this as well as ideas and activities on how to look for color inspiration in the resource guide.

My Color Story

I've always gravitated towards thick black lines and bright colors, so when I started my sketchnoting and graphic recording journey those were the colors I used. Then one day I attended a workshop with other graphic recorders and the presenter advised us not to use black, suggesting that it's too harsh. Suddenly I felt embarrassed by my natural color style!

For a while, I tried not using much black at all, but it just didn't feel right. Thankfully, I soon realized that color preferences are PERSONAL. Your color choices and how you use them are completely up to you! Sometimes I'll use dark grays and blues instead but I still love to use bright colors and lots of black. Do what feels good to you!

Consider Branding and Themes

Maybe you work for a company that has brand colors. You could certainly use those in your sketchnote. If you're at a conference and sketchnoting a presentation for yourself, you could use the colors that the speaker uses on their slides.

Get Subtle with Shades and Tones

You can also choose to stick with a monochromatic palette (a variety of shades, tones, and tints of a single color). A tint is when you make a color lighter. A shade is when you make a color darker. And tones are when you make the color brighter or duller.

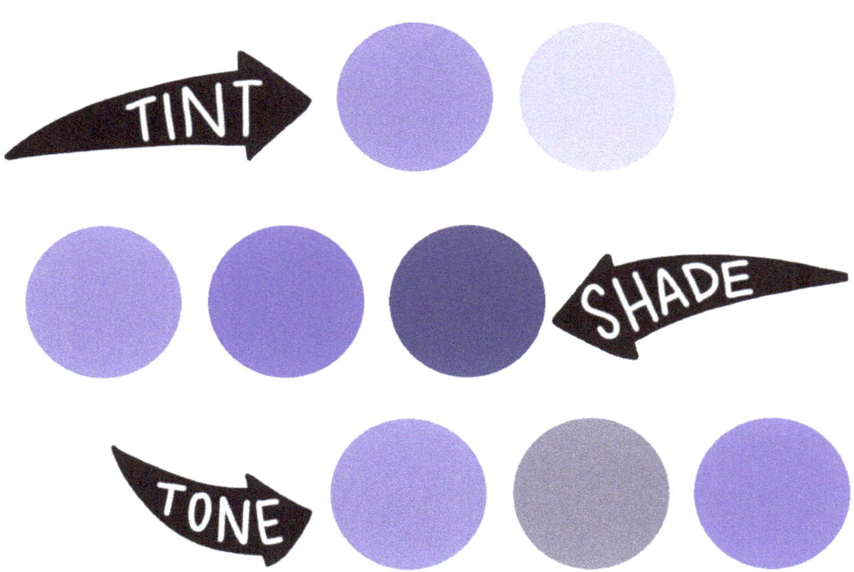

Play around with tints, shades, and tones. This option may work better when working digitally because the sky's the limit when it comes to color choice—but if you have enough markers, you can manage it on paper too!

EXERCISE

Play with palettes

Your choice of palette is entirely up to you! Here are some ideas to try as you practice your sketchnotes—play with them and see how it goes!

1. Base your choice of color on the theme of the presentation. Is the presentation about nature? Try greens, browns, and blues.

2. Use the presenter's visual aids to help you choose a style and palette for your sketchnote.

3. Challenge yourself to create a sketchnote using only two colors (your main writing color plus ONE more).

You Don't Have to Color in the Whole Thing

Fully coloring in drawings can take a long time, and time can be in short supply when you're sketchnoting!

One shortcut I learned is to outline a shape in the color of the object as well as in black. If I drew an apple I might color the outline in red instead of coloring in the whole thing. That shows the reader that it's a red apple without taking the extra time that solid coloring would.

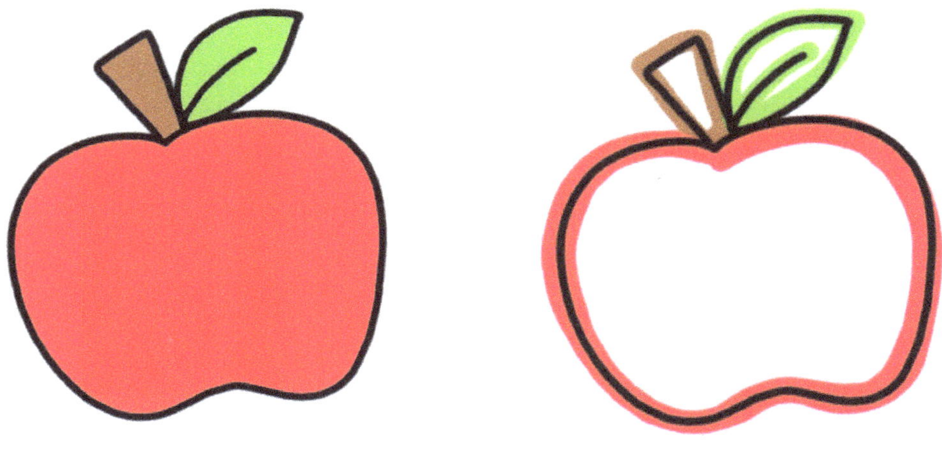

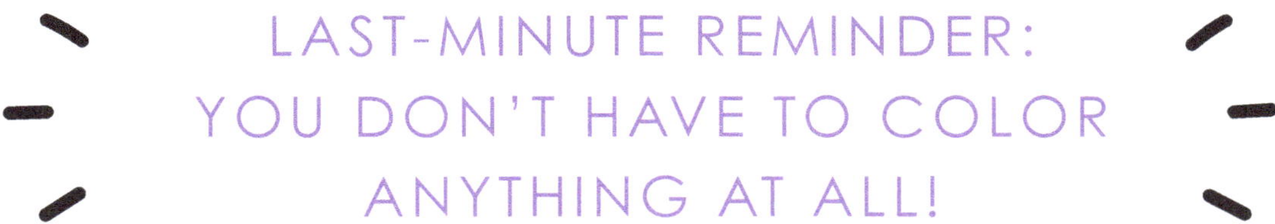

Keep in mind that your sketchnote is still 100% valid if you opt not to add any color whatsoever! You can also sketchnote the whole thing in your main color and then go back and add other colors later. Don't let perfectionism tell you any different. Do what feels good!

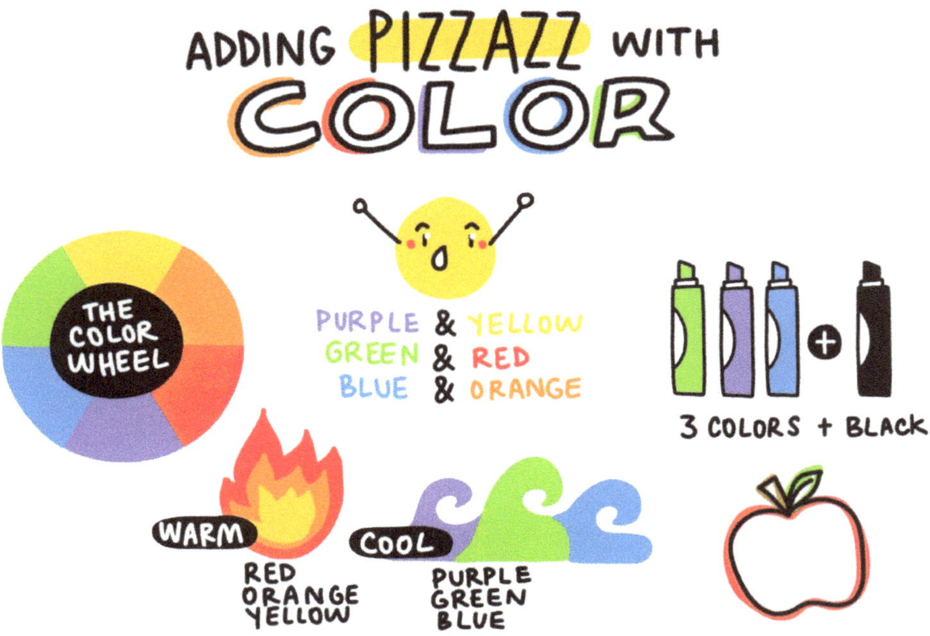

For this sketchnote, you can see how I brought the overarching themes and ideas together. You'll notice that I didn't write the words "complementary colors" but rather chose to draw a "Wow!" face to express that "wow" factor that we talked about. You can also notice that I didn't write anything about the idea of coloring the outline of the image, but I used the same example in the book. This simple image should jog my memory about that technique.

A Sketchnote is the Thing You Create, Sketchnoting is the Act of Creating (And Both Are Important)

So far, you've learned many of the major elements of a sketchnote, but you're possibly still feeling like you don't really know HOW to sketchnote. Here's why: "Sketchnote" is a noun AND a verb.

A sketchnote, the noun, uses text and graphics to synthesize and summarize information. A sketchnote (n.) combines the elements from Part One to make a finished piece—you can look at it afterward and pick out each element to see how it was used (Note: this can be a fun learning activity!).

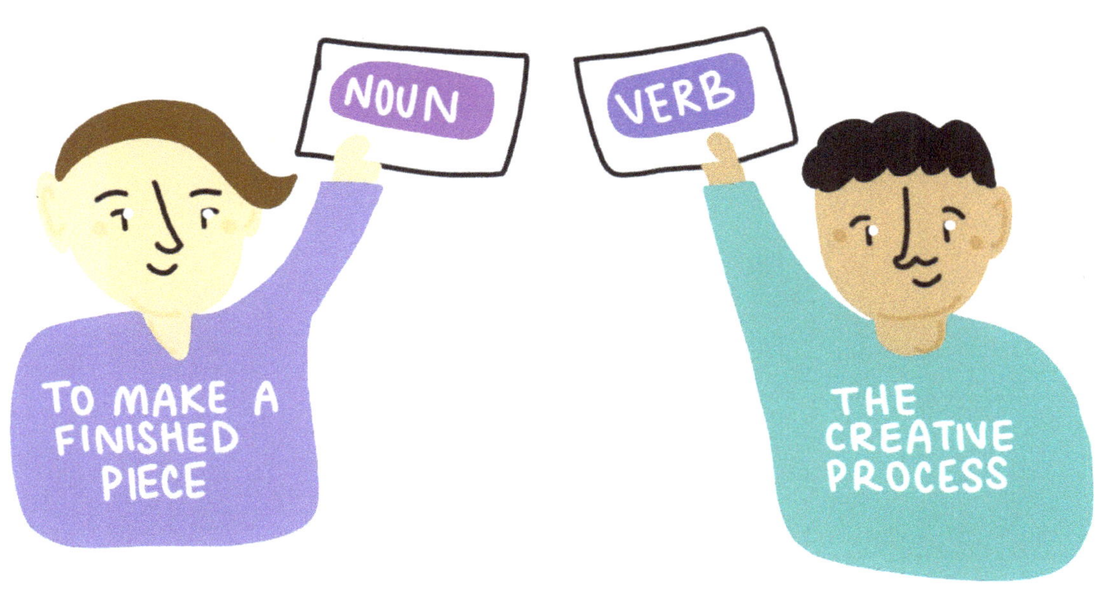

Learning the elements in Part One first will help you start putting pen to paper and build your confidence as you practice. I separated the different techniques and elements into steps to make them clearer. You can (and should!) practice each step in this book until you get more comfortable with them.

However, when you're ready to sit down and practice creating a full sketchnote, you can use the elements in whatever order you need them. You'll start with Step 1 ... but after that the process will be intuitive.

And that's where sketchnote, the verb comes in.

Part 2 is designed to help you shift your focus from the elements that go into a sketchnote (the noun) to the process of sketchnoting (the verb). I've included tips for figuring out what to capture (which is a question I get asked all the time) as well as ideas for how to combine elements you learned earlier to communicate ideas effectively.

Note: Because this second part introduces just a few processes instead of a collection of elements, you'll notice that it's shorter than Part One. That doesn't mean it's less important—just that most of what you need to learn here is based on concepts and strategies instead of how-tos and step-by-step instructions.

Extra Special Note: The true magic of sketchnoting is in the process! Don't get hung up on trying to create a completely perfect-looking sketchnote, especially when you're starting out. You'll do your best learning through creating. Let yourself play and see what happens!

PART TWO

The Sketchnoting Process

The Sketchnoting Process Explained

Now that you have an idea of what goes into a sketchnote, it's time to dig into how it all works in practice. "But *how* do I sketchnote?" is a question that I hear a lot, and trust me, I've given the answer a TON of thought!

In this section, I'll break down the different activities involved in sketchnoting, give you plenty of tips to help make practice easy and fun, and finish with some "lab experiments" for you to play with. Ready? Let's explore!

Sketchnoting, the verb, is the act of translating spoken words into a visual message. It's more than simply writing and drawing—when you're sketchnoting, you're doing several things at once. Here's what the sketchnoting process involves:

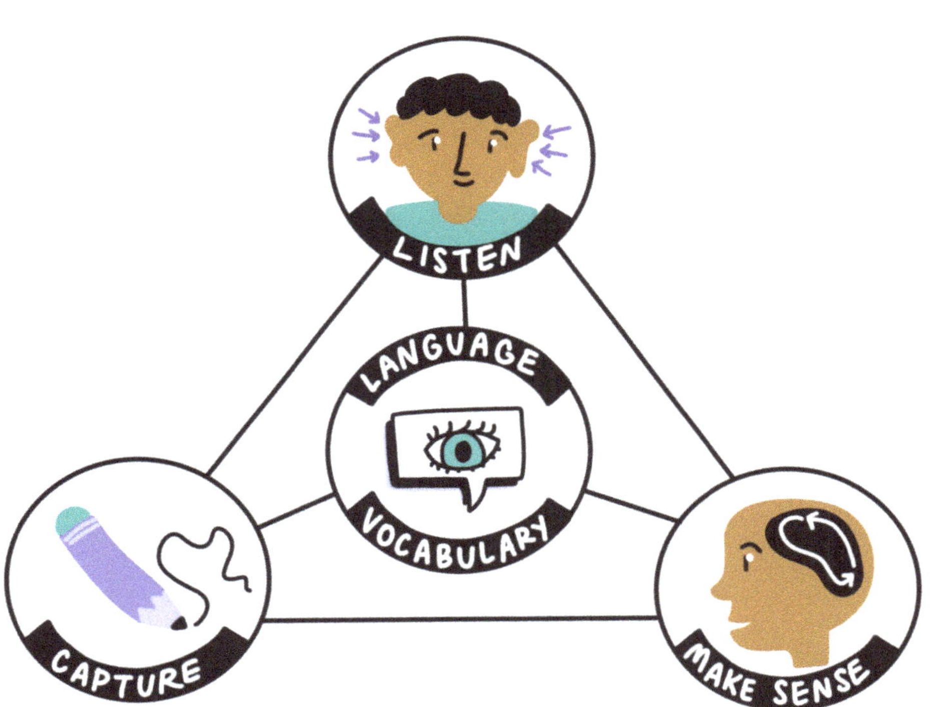

Here's a quick rundown of what you're looking at:

- ☑ Listening is actively paying attention to the information that's presented.

- ☑ Making Sense is synthesizing the information and figuring out what to include in your sketchnote.

- ☑ Capturing is recording that information on your page.

- ☑ The circle in the middle represents the written and visual languages that you use to capture what you've heard and made sense of. The combination of written and visual vocabulary is at the heart of sketchnoting (Confused? Don't worry, we'll dig into it later).

And when you sketchnote (v.) you're doing these things simultaneously.

The keyword is *simultaneously*. You're not doing one thing at a time, ever (or at least not for long).

Sound scary? Let out that breath you're holding, and keep in mind that you do things simultaneously *all the time*. You walk and chew gum. You eat and watch TV. You have wild kitchen dance parties while you cook supper (just me?). You, my friend, have *got* this!

Like I've said before, you can't do this wrong—but you CAN make things easier for yourself by trying to balance the different activities. If you listen to information for too long before starting to make sense of what you're hearing, you're bound to forget some details. If you focus too much on capturing and adding a ton of embellishments, you may miss vital information. And so on.

Keep in mind that a lot of sketchnoting is intuitive. You have to hear what stands out as important and capture what feels right. It's called "making sense" because it needs to make sense for YOU. This process can take some getting used to but it sounds more complicated than it actually is.

We're going to look at the different activities one at a time. Remember: I'm breaking these elements down separately so that each one is easier to understand, and not because you actually *do* these things separately.

If any of this feels hard or overwhelming, please know: you're not doing it "wrong." You're not "bad at it." You're *learning*. You're using your brain in new ways. It takes some getting used to. That's why practicing is key—not just drawing the individual elements from Part One, but actively sketchnoting.

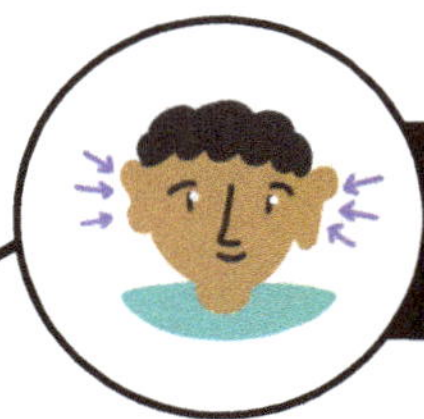

LISTENING

Listening is a huge part of sketchnoting. Sometimes I even refer to myself as a professional listener. If I'm not listening to everything (and I mean everything) then I could miss important information to capture in the graphic.

As you practice sketchnoting, you'll become a master listener. Listening attentively makes the rest of the sketchnoting process possible. You need to do more than simply *hear* the words the speaker says—you need to *understand* them.

I'm sure you've been in a situation before where you were speaking to someone but they weren't fully paying attention. You can often tell by what their next response is: they'll only pick up on the surface meaning or understand part of what you said. It's your job to avoid this.

To fully grasp the meaning at the heart of what the speaker is saying, you need to practice active listening. Give the speaker your full attention, with the goal of fully absorbing and understanding what they're saying. Really take it all in and remember that active listening is more than just hearing the words someone says.

Even when you're capturing information on your page, make sure you glance up regularly so you can take in what the speaker is doing. Pay attention to the way the speaker or teacher moves. Also, notice their tone of voice, any intentional pauses, the *way* they're speaking. You may get clues that help you understand the meaning more completely.

If you do find your mind wandering, be kind to yourself and gently bring your attention back to what you're doing. If you find yourself getting tired, and you have the option, give yourself a break for a few minutes and then come back to what you're sketchnoting.

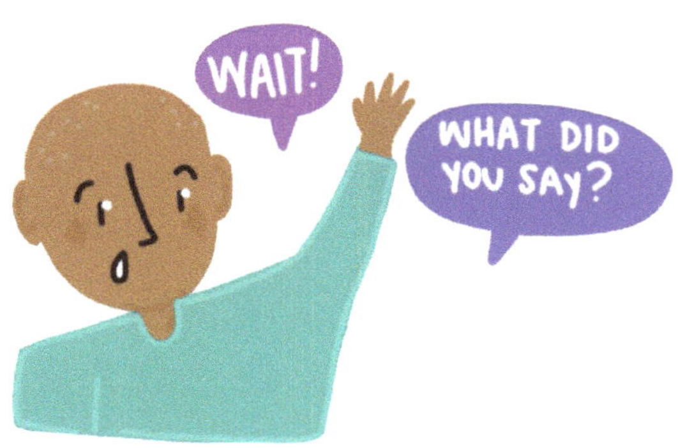

Tips for Setting Yourself Up to Listen

Before I sketchnote, I take a minute to get my bearings and make sure I'm ready to focus. It doesn't take long and it makes a huge difference.

Here are some questions to consider before you begin:

Do you have everything that you need in order to sit for a period of time?
Do you have all your materials? Enough paper? Markers? Pencil and eraser?
Do you have some water close by so you can stay hydrated?
Are you well rested?

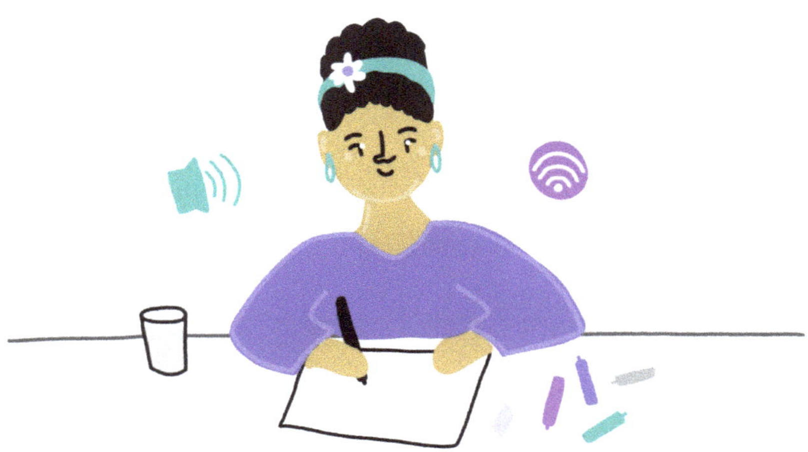

Take your environment into consideration. Some folks can't concentrate when they are sitting at a messy desk. Can you take two minutes and do a quick tidy so that you can focus?

If you're sketchnoting at home, is your internet connection reliable?
Does your computer's sound work well?

If you're sketchnoting an in-person class, meeting, or conference,
can you see the speaker and/or any visual aids?

You know yourself better than I do! Take a moment to prepare yourself properly so that you can be successful in your sketchnoting session.

Listening and Making Sense: Different Skills Working Together

When you consider the sketchnoting process, "listening" and "making sense" go hand in hand. Picture your brain as a funnel, with a large opening at the top and narrowing to a small opening at the bottom (see the graphic below). All the information you hear and see goes into the top of the funnel.

Then the ideas need to be compressed and simplified to fit through the bottom of the funnel and make it onto the page.

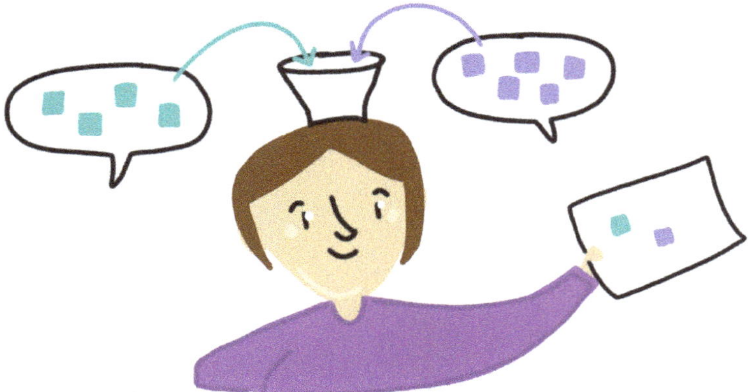

Remember: You DON'T have to capture every bit of information. Sitting and listening for the first few minutes of a presentation—or in the middle, especially if you are feeling overwhelmed—is not just OK, it's encouraged. Sometimes pausing for a moment, so that you can make sense of what you're hearing, is at least as useful as (and often *more* useful than frantically capturing.

According to studies cited by educational psychologist Jerome Bruner of New York University, adding visuals boosts memory from 10% (listening only) to 80% (seeing and doing) so that you actually retain the information presented.[9]

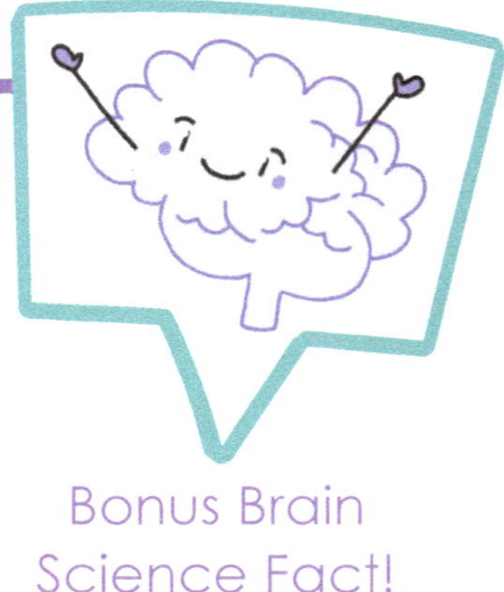

When you're making sense of what you hear, you're distilling the message to its most important parts so you know what to capture. It's the part that beginners often find the most intimidating (right up there with straight lines and stick figures!).

Luckily, most presenters (or books, videos, articles, or whatever else you want to sketchnote) don't make you do all the work. There are cues you can listen for that will give you hints about what's important and what can be skipped.

Content Cues to Watch Out For

1. **The Set Up: "I'm going to tell you the 5 steps to ..."**
   You'll be surprised how often this happens. Speakers love to give you a preview of their structure. Listen for "the X steps to" or "the Y factors in," or "the Z causes of." This will help you get a sense of how to structure your sketchnote.

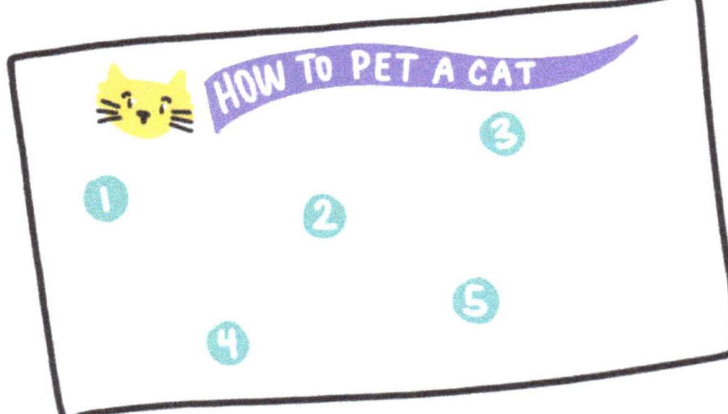

2. **People Summarizing Themselves: "What I'm really trying to say is ..."**
   Sketchnoting is all about active listening and assessing in the moment whether you need to include a piece of information. Always listen for a verbal cue that indicates an incoming summary, especially after an anecdote or more involved story that you might have chosen not to capture. Often, the speaker will do the work for you and give you the perfect piece of information to include in your sketchnote.

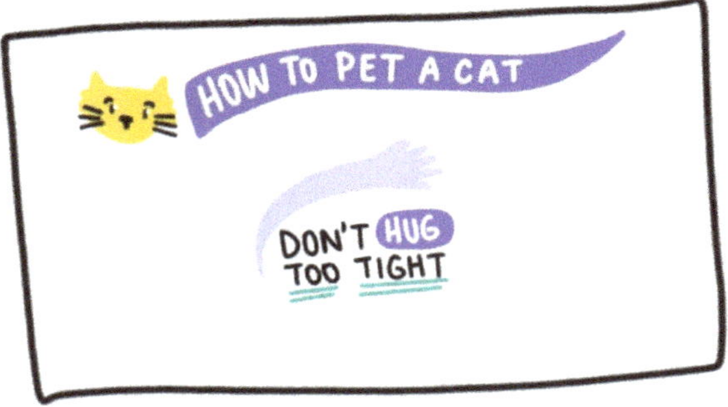

3. **Emphasis: Listen for the way the person is speaking. Pronunciation and emotions.**

    Keep an ear out for changes in the way the presenter speaks. Are they adding extra emphasis to something? The way they speak can give you clues about how important that information is.

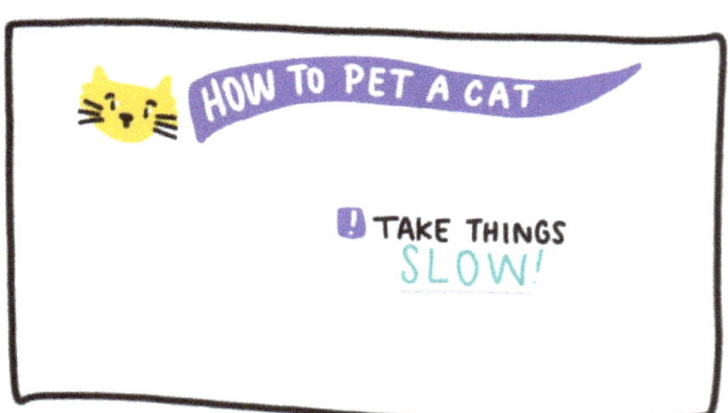

4. **The Moral of the Story: "And that's why you should always ..."**

    People are natural storytellers, so you'll come across this quite often. If the person is telling a story, take a pause and listen for the crucial lesson.

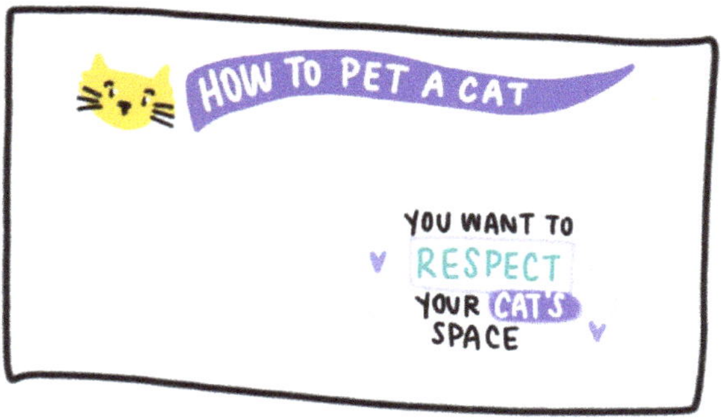

Dealing with Unfamiliar Topics

Sometimes you might find yourself creating a sketchnote about a completely new-to-you topic. If that's the case, don't panic! Remember why you're there in the first place. You may be interested in the topic and want to learn more, maybe you're exploring a new career path, or taking a class. You don't have to be an expert in the field to create effective sketchnotes.

If you're completely new with absolutely no prior knowledge, you could consider doing a bit of homework beforehand. Read some articles or watch some YouTube videos to help you get comfortable with the subject and terminology. Note: You absolutely do not have to do this, it's just an idea that can help if you're feeling nervous!

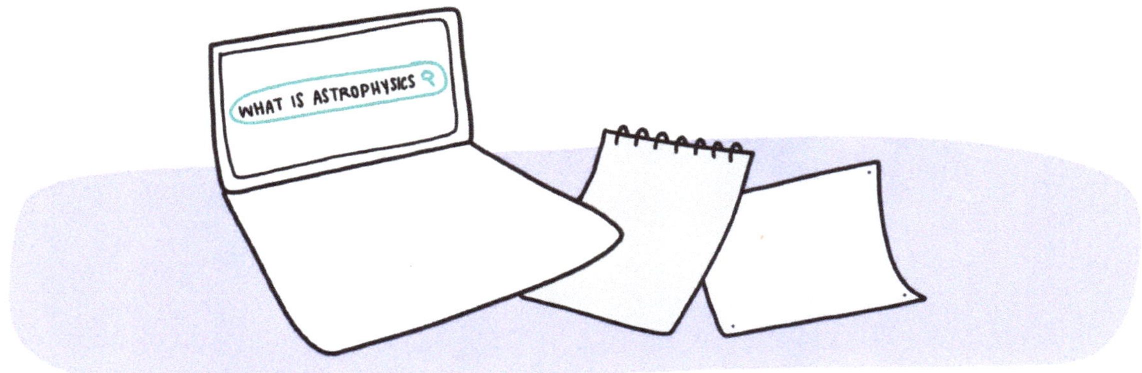

Unfamiliar topics may result in a messier sketchnote, and that's ok. You might have to write down an acronym and go and research what it is later. Don't worry too much about what you don't know! Creating your sketchnote will help remind you about what to explore later.

If you're really struggling, you could write your notes in bullet point format during the class or presentation and then go back later and create a sketchnote based on them. Reviewing the information this way can help you get more familiar with it as well as giving you time to work out the best way to capture it in a sketchnote.

Determining What's Important

If you're sketchnoting a topic that you're highly familiar with, you may have a clear idea of what's important. That can really come in handy. But if the topic is less familiar, honestly, you might not know what's important. Do your best to read the speaker's cues—and if everything else fails, take your best guess. Onward!

Notice Your Own A-Ha Moments:

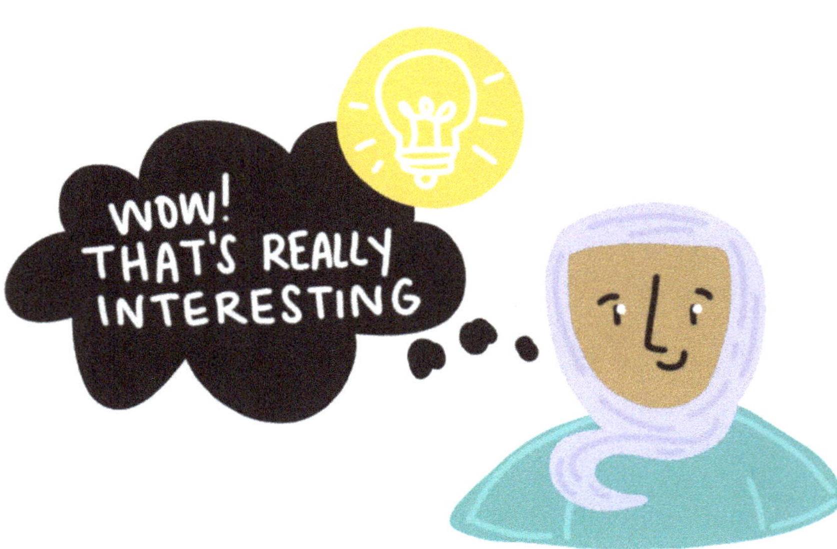

Pay attention to your own reactions to the information you hear. Your own insights and a-ha moments add to your experience and can help enrich your understanding later on.

Sometimes it's Hard ... And That's Not Your Fault!

In a perfect world, every speaker would be engaging and organized. They'd cue the important points and use emphasis and significant pauses to highlight key information. Sadly, not every speaker does this. And when they don't, all you can do is your best.

One time I was hired to do a live graphic recording for a super-famous speaker in front of a massive audience. And he was, frankly, terrible. I just carried on and did what I could ... and the next day the conference organizers told me they felt bad for me up there. It is what it is.

If you're in a situation like this, try not to panic! Just keep trying to make sense of what the speaker is saying and capture it. Remember that you'd feel just as lost (if not more so) if you were trying to write everything down word for word.

The good news is that it gets easier with practice! I've had people come up to me at conferences and tell me that they can't believe what I ended up drawing ... because they didn't understand a word the speaker said!

A study of high school students and industrial workers conducted by Australian psychologist John Sweller found that visual language produces better problem solving. Subjects got 45% of the answers correct on a test using conventional text and separate diagrams vs. 64% of the answers correct using integrated text and diagrams. Visual language produces higher retention (22% more) and in less time (13% less.)[10]

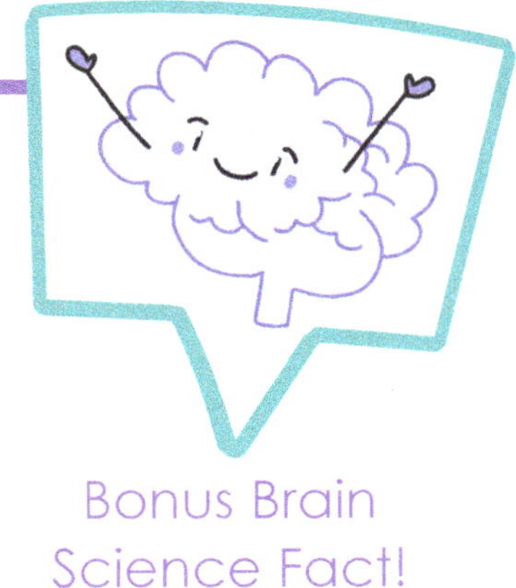

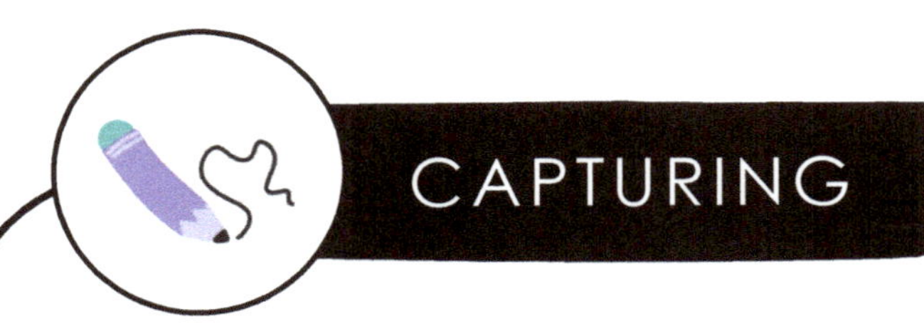

While listening and making sense happen in your brain, capturing is where the pen meets the paper. Now, we covered a ton of the elements of a sketchnote in Part One, so you already have a handle on the tools we use to capture information. Because of that, this section is going to focus more on tips, troubleshooting, and addressing concerns that beginner sketchnoters bring up all the time.

Newer sketchnoters tend to worry that they'll fall behind, capture the wrong thing, or mess up their sketchnote because they made the wrong call. Here are some tips to set your mind at ease:

Practical Tips for Capturing

1. **Keep Scrap Paper or Sticky Notes on Hand**.
   If you're unsure of whether a piece of information needs to be captured, or if you're waiting to see where it fits, you can jot things down on sticky notes or small pieces of paper.

   I recommend using multiple papers so that you can choose some and toss others aside easily. Don't feel like you have to use everything you write down!

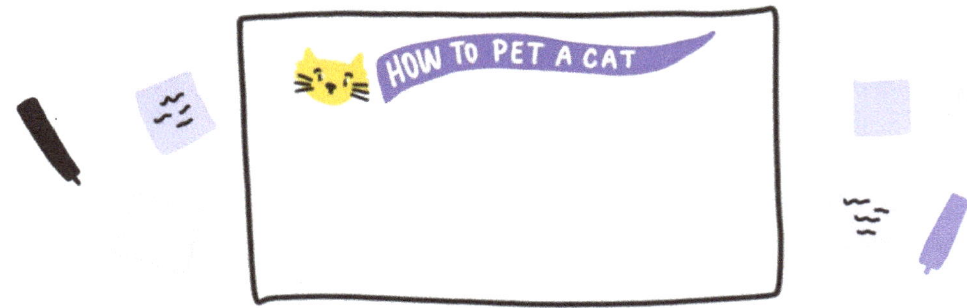

2. **Use the Start and Come Back Method.**
   If you're in a rush, start drawing a thing or writing a word and give yourself permission to move on before it's done. Then go back after the presentation is over and fill in the missing information.

As long as you have a clear idea of what you need to fill in *and you actually do it*, you're all set. This method is also great for times when you're not sure how to spell a word or a name. Write the few letters you're sure of, then go back later and fill in the rest.

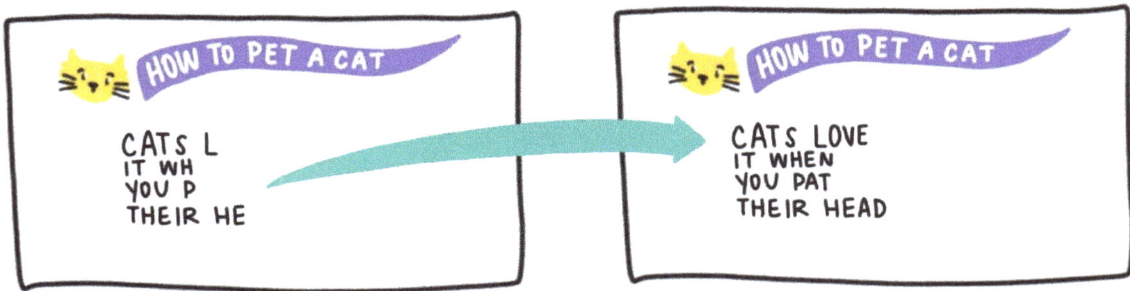

3. **Keep in Mind That There are Multiple Ways to Make Your Point.**
   Say you're happily capturing a presentation ... when suddenly you realize that the point you thought was just another minor piece of information was actually Hugely Important. You remember that you're "supposed to" write big ideas, big and small ideas, small ... but you wrote this big point in small writing! What do you do?

   Breathe. You're fine. You can use containers, underlines, embellishment, or color to draw attention to the point and show that it's important. Try to shift your approach from "Oh no! I messed up!" to "OK ... how can I make this work?

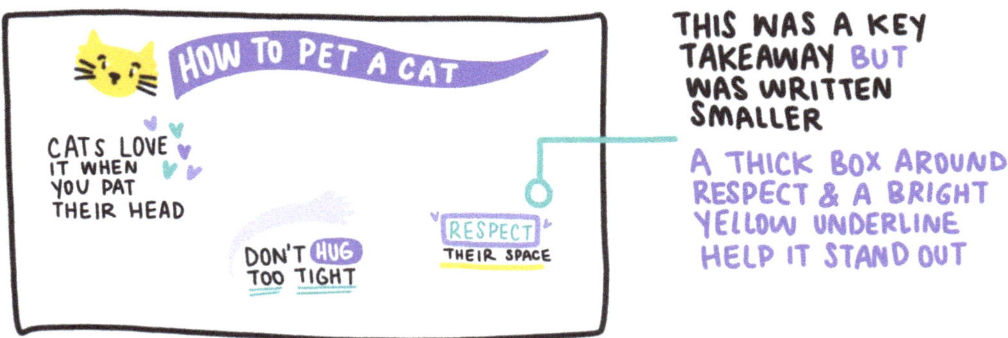

4. **Less is More.**

I mentioned storytelling in the "making sense" section, so let's revisit that as an example of "less is more." I'll often write out the main lesson of a story with a small drawing to go with it, instead of capturing the entirety of the plot. Writing out the conclusion or a key takeaway from it helps me remember other pieces of the story beyond what I've captured. This is some of the magic behind sketchnoting.

How can you say what you need to say in the fewest words possible?
Can you take away some filler words while still getting the point across?

Find ways, in the moment, to cut corners. Don't feel like you have to write out full sentences. Give yourself permission to leave out punctuation. If you're sketchnoting very quickly, focus on the essentials and decide if some things can wait till the end when you're finishing up.

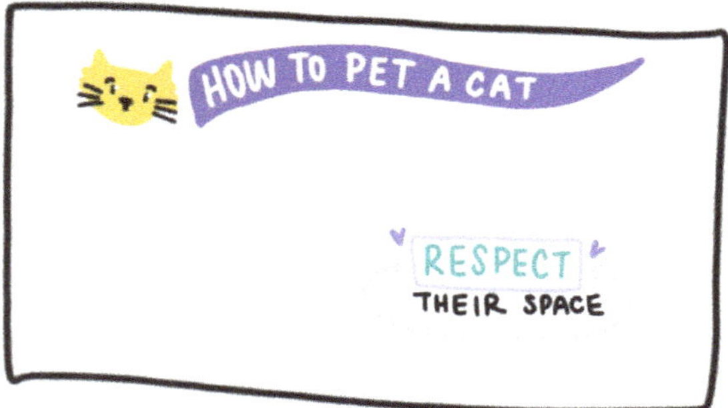

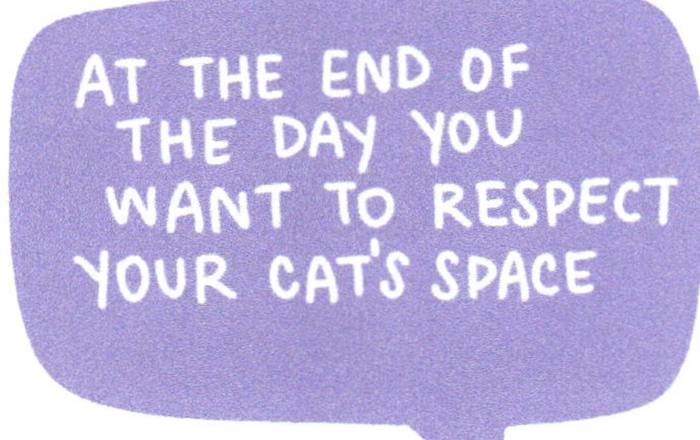

5. **More Writing or More Drawing?**

Each person is going to have their own unique style of sketchnoting. I've seen sketchnotes that are highly illustrative with very few words and I've seen them where there are hardly any drawings at all!

When I have the opportunity to teach sketchnoting in person with a group of people and we share our finished sketchnotes with each other, it's still always amazing to me how unique and different they are. The balance between drawing and writing is such an individual choice!

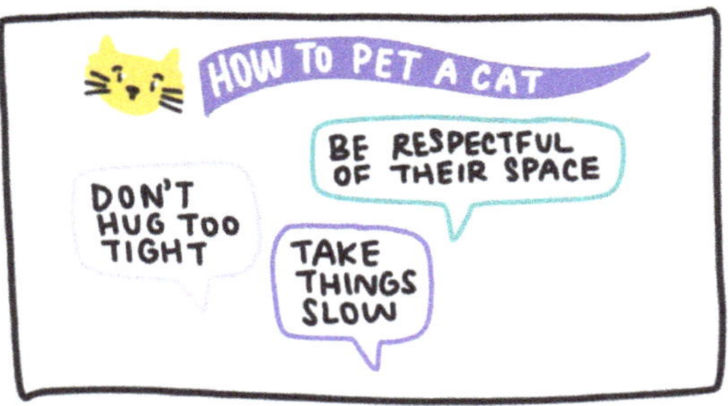

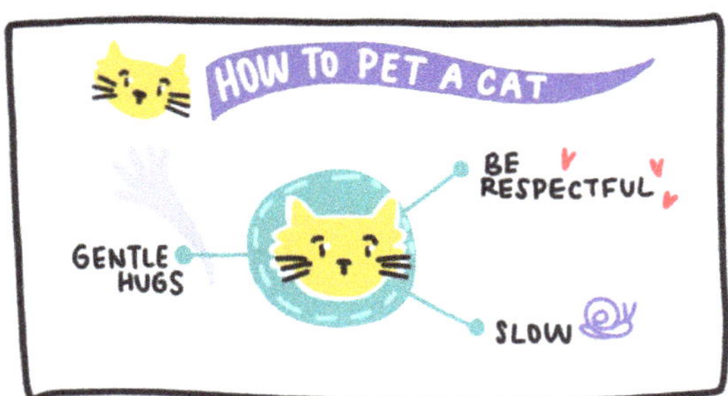

Dealing with "Mistakes"

Embrace the Idea of Happy Accidents.

I love the quote from painting teacher, TV personality, and beloved cultural icon Bob Ross: "We don't make mistakes, we have happy accidents." There is so much truth in this when it comes to sketchnoting.

Often when I feel like I've made a mistake, I wind up turning that "mistake" into something that I hadn't even considered. Some of my favorite style decisions started off with something I didn't intentionally mean to put down on the page. When you make what you think is a mistake, see what you can turn that into!

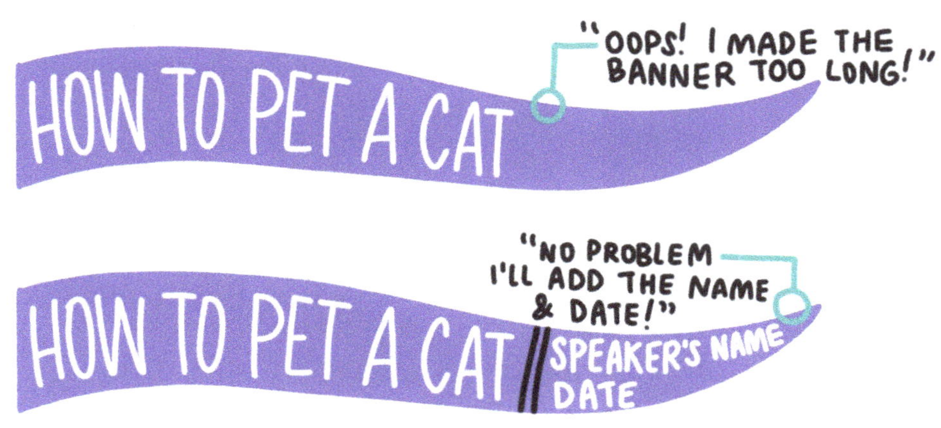

Did You Spell Something Wrong?

As a professional graphic recorder, I spell things wrong all the time. We aren't human dictionaries, so don't let the fact that you don't know how to spell something trip you up. In sketchnoting, time is often of the essence, and speed matters. If you don't know how to spell a word, just do the best you can and, if you want, come back and fix it at a later date.

To help you remember to come back, and to infuse your sketchnote with a little bit of playfulness, grab a red pen or marker and draw a red squiggly line under the word, similar to how word processing spell checkers do on the computer.

Bonus: If you keep at it, sketchnoting will probably make you a better speller!

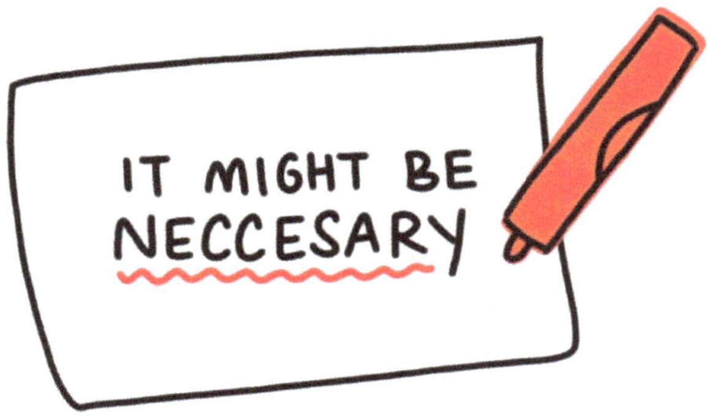

Use Address Labels to Erase Mistakes You Can't Embrace

If you're using pens, markers, or something that you can't erase, keep address labels (printable white paper labels you can buy at office supply stores) in your bag. That way you can cut or rip off the size that you need and stick it over top of any mistakes you can't work with. Address labels are perfect because they aren't glossy, so they're easy to write on!

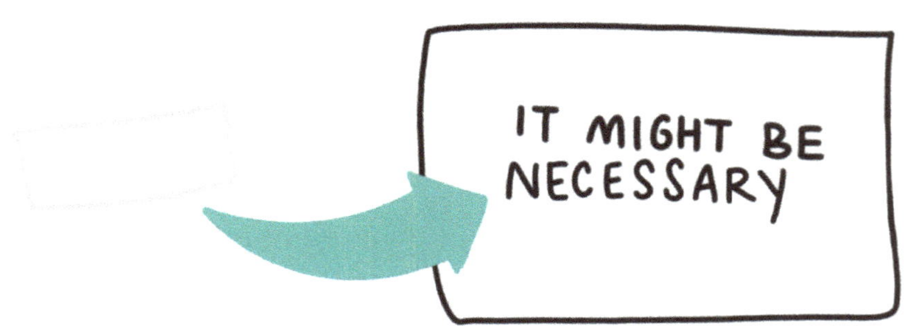

SKETCHNOTING USES A VISUAL LANGUAGE— AND YOU CAN PRACTICE IT!

At its most basic level, language is using one thing to represent another. For example, the spoken word "chair" or the letters c-h-a-i-r are symbols for the actual, physical thing in my living room. And if you think about sign language—there's a specific gesture that represents the word "chair." That's another kind of symbol.

When we sketchnote, we do the same thing—but we can also use the *drawing* of a chair as the symbol. Drawing is a visual language that we use to support, clarify, or expand the meaning of carefully chosen words.

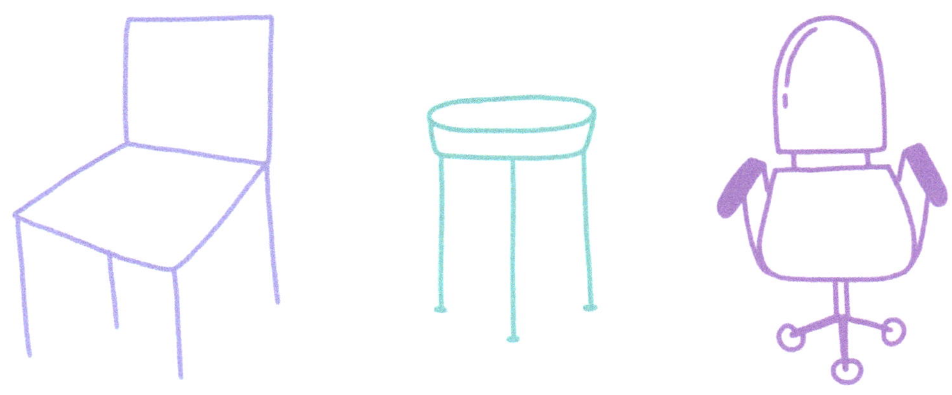

Visual Language Has a Vocabulary That You Can Practice

What happens when you start learning a new language? You learn a few words and the basic way to use them, but whenever you try to say something new you have to pause and mentally sort through the words you know so you can figure out how to *say the thing*.

Then as you practice, you *add the words to your vocabulary*. At first, you may have to think for a minute about what word to use for "chair," but if you keep practicing, it won't take any conscious thought—the word will just come to you.

And what's more, with practice you'll also be able to access the words "armchair," "recliner," "rocker," and "stool" (and more!) just as quickly and know immediately which one fits the context.

This happens in sketchnoting as well. You can *add images to your visual vocabulary* so that the next time a speaker says "chair," rocker," or "stool," you'll know immediately what to draw and how to draw it *without even thinking about it.*

Building visual vocabulary is just like playing scales on an instrument or sitting down to meditate every day: you have to do the work to reap the rewards. But it's so worth it when you're sketchnoting and the pictures come easily. That's why I'm going to get you started with some icons that you can practice right away. Keep working on them until you can picture them immediately and you feel confident drawing them.

In a study by the University of Waterloo, subjects were given a list of 30 words. They had 40 seconds per word to either write it repeatedly or draw it. They were later asked to recall as many words as they could in just 60 seconds. Subjects consistently remembered the drawn words better—in fact, in some cases they remembered twice as many drawn words as written ones. Also (and this is important) *the quality of the drawings didn't matter.* This worked even when they had just 4 seconds to draw each word![11]

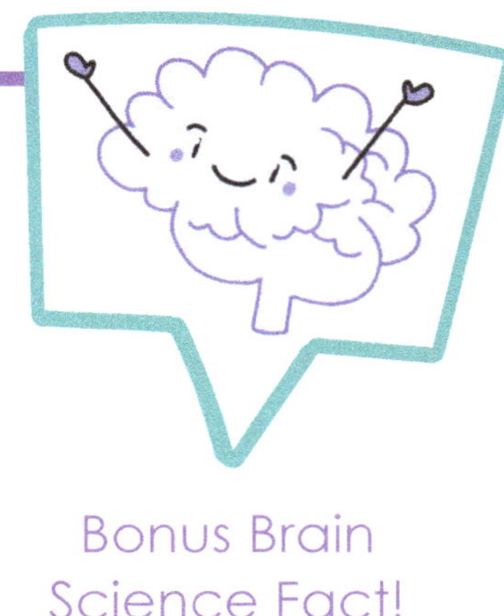

Bonus Brain Science Fact!

You Can Communicate Complex Ideas Quickly

With practice, you'll develop a collection of icons you can use to represent more complicated ideas and topics. For example, I've done approximately a zillion graphic recording sessions for presentations about cyber security. I've built a very specific visual vocabulary around this topic. So now if someone says "adversary," my hands already know exactly what to draw.

15 Visual Icons to Add to Your Vocabulary

I went through my catalog of graphic recordings and came up with a list of 15 common icons that are fairly simple to draw and can be used to express a variety of meanings. I've included some ideas of different uses for each icon so you can see the possibilities.

I've also included step-by-step drawings so you can see exactly how to create them (and then you can practice them—again, don't forget to practice!). Remember that you don't have to copy my drawings exactly, though! Feel free to change the look of these however you like.

Magnifying glass
Can represent: focus, magnify, research, inspect, analyze, identity, examine

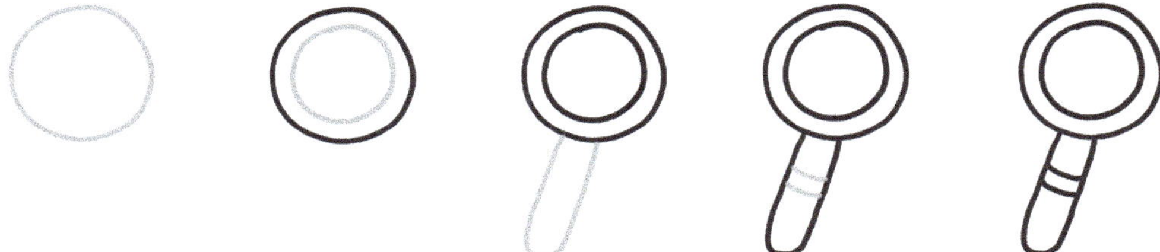

Lightbulb
Can represent: idea, a-ha moment, highlight something important, understand, innovation

Location marker
Can represent: location, journey, start here, map, track, destination

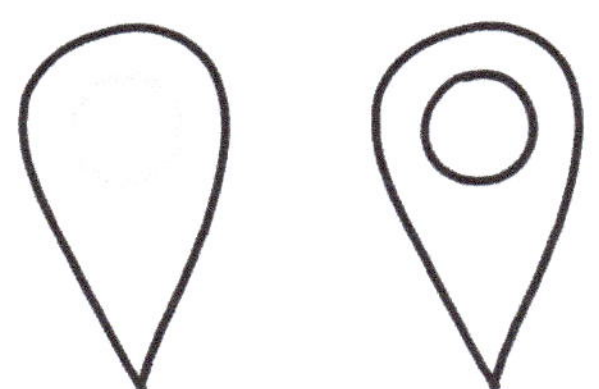

Pencil

Can represent: draw, write, picture, script, notes, create

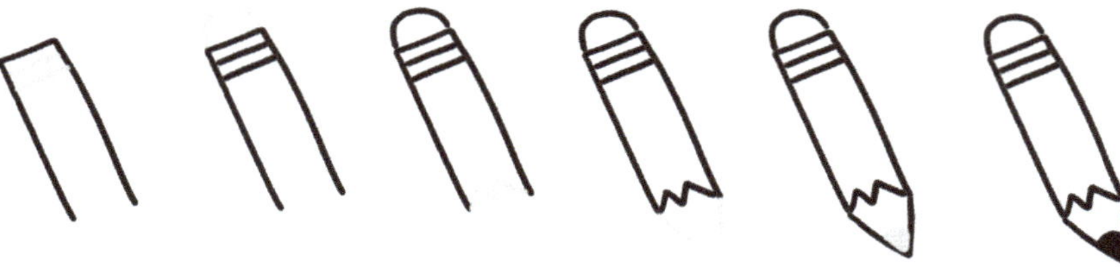

Letter

Can represent: message, text, notice, communication, email, contact

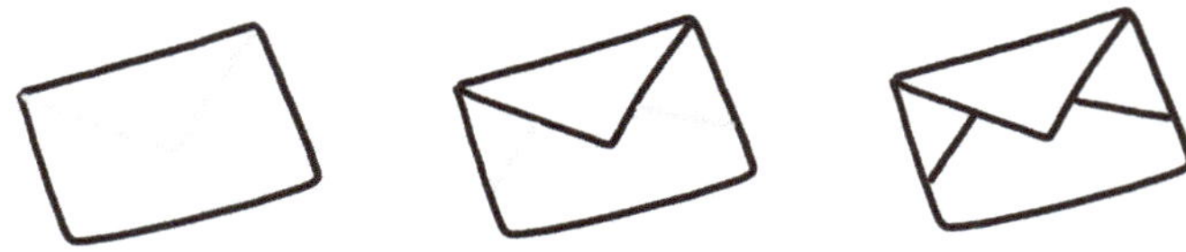

Clock

Can represent: time, watch, patience

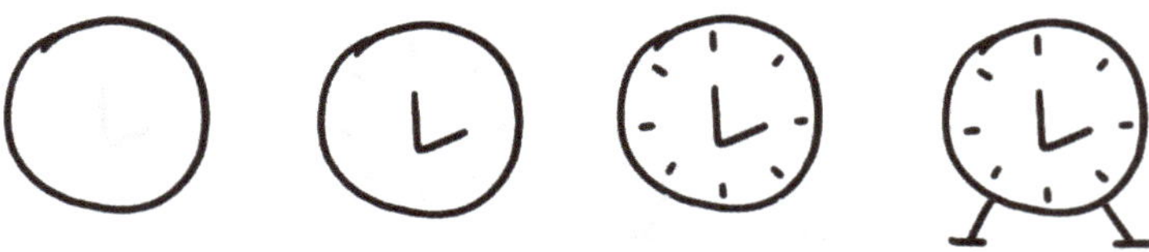

Seedling

Can represent: growth, something emerging, from the ground up, sustainability, bloom

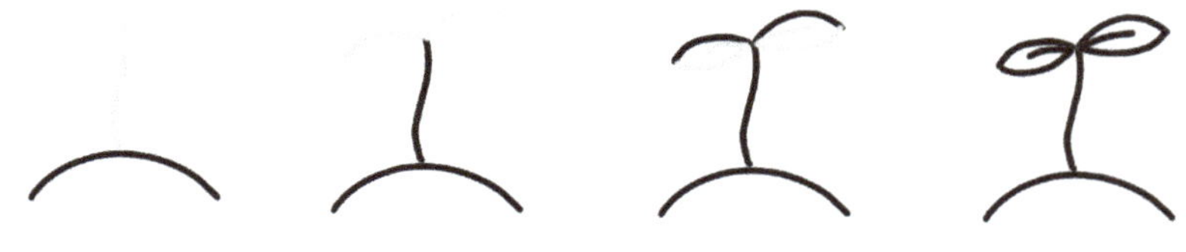

Eye

Can represent: visualization, see, vision, look, observe, aware, perception

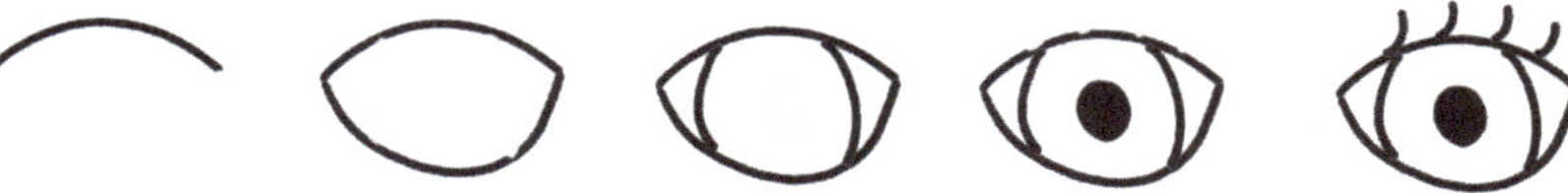

Puzzle piece

Can represent: solve, game, fitting together, complexity

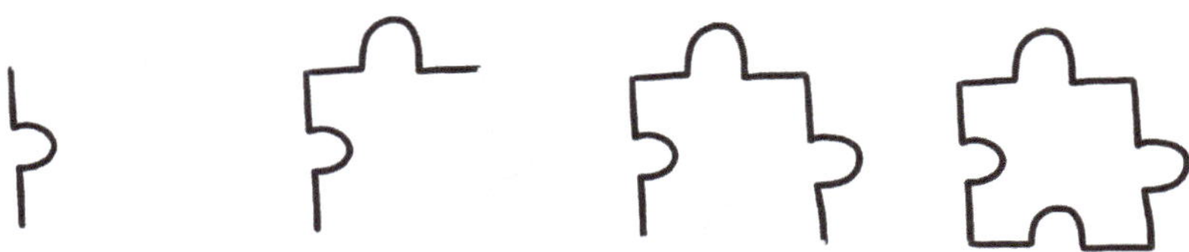

Spaceship

Can represent: launch, discover, space, future, reach for the stars, visionary, dream, galaxy

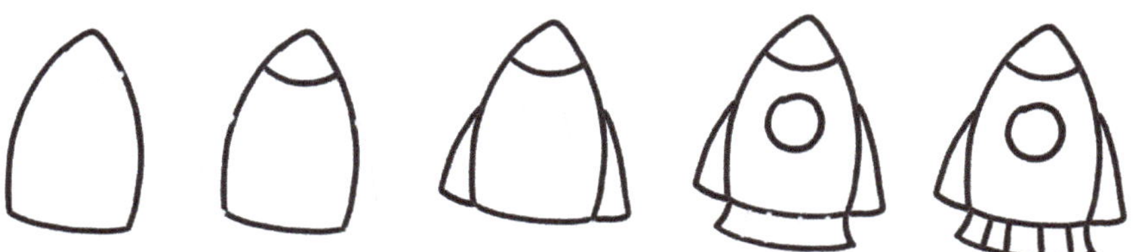

Open book

Can represent: learn, knowledge, read, study, gain

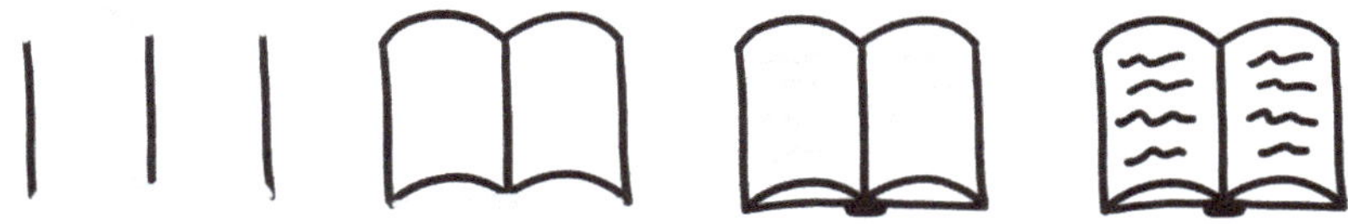

Laptop

Can represent: technology, computer, work, remote, mechanics

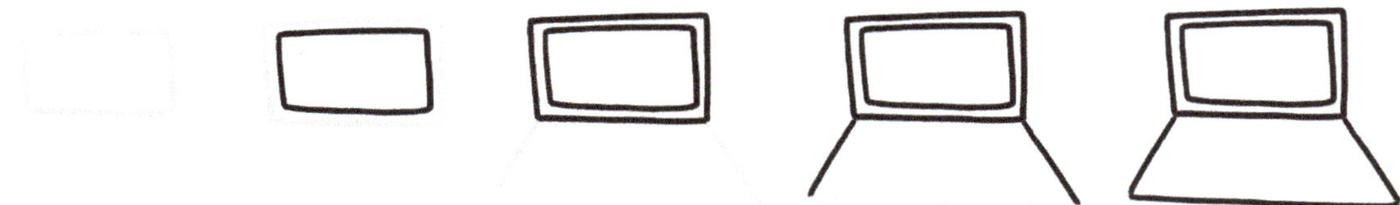

Lock

Can represent: unlocking or locking of ideas, security, protect, key ideas, safety, defend

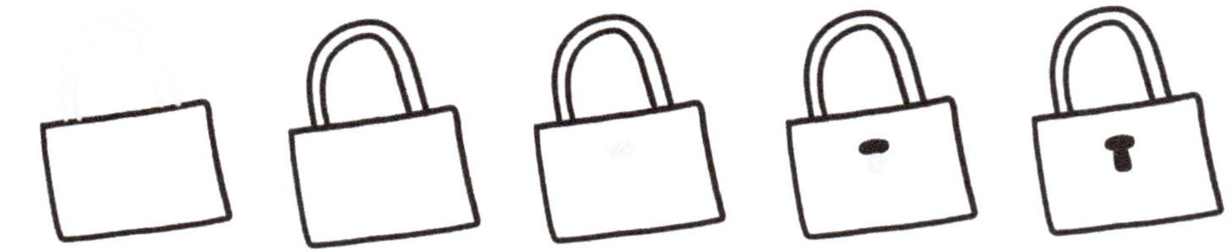

Jewel

Can represent: value or values, quality, luxury, precious, something valuable and meaningful

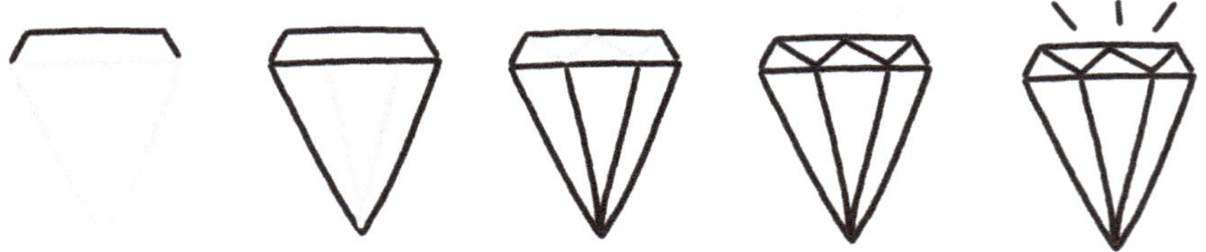

Target

Can represent: goals, strategy, reaching for something, objective

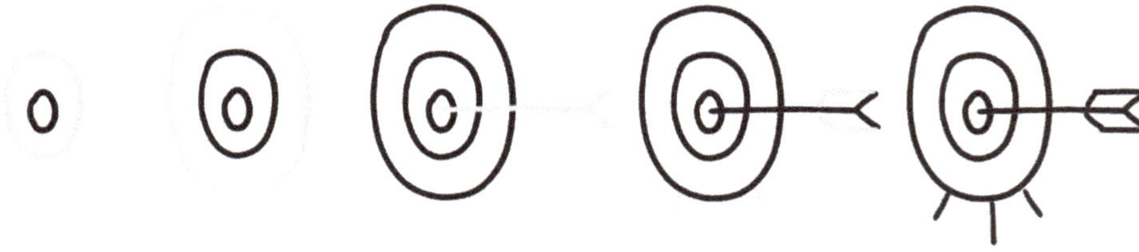

Note that there are 15 icons here ... but if you count out each of the possible meanings, you're looking at 80+ different concepts that you can communicate with them.

Looking for more visual inspiration? Check the link to my online Resource Guide—I keep it up to date with my own sketchnoting information and other websites to check out.

IMPORTANT: Be Aware of Tokens and Culturally Inappropriate Drawings

I was recently graphic facilitating an online session where I had pre-drawn a few elements as a request from my client. One of those elements was a flag on a hill or mountain. I used this fairly often to represent reaching a goal or destination, or something to strive towards.

However, during the session a kind person privately messaged me to say that, while having a mission is great, using imagery of planting flags on land is seen as a symbol of dominance and colonial violence by many marginalized communities.

Once she pointed it out, I couldn't believe that I hadn't realized it before! I appreciated that she had been kind enough to let me know, and told her so. She made an alternative suggestion as well and while we were on a short break I quickly changed the drawing.

Unconscious bias is so insidious and it takes work to counteract. Avoid drawing anything that could be seen or perceived as stereotypes. This could include clothing items or common symbols for a specific culture. And if someone points out something you're drawing that's unintentionally harmful, be open to the feedback. Don't be hard on yourself, but see it as a teaching moment.

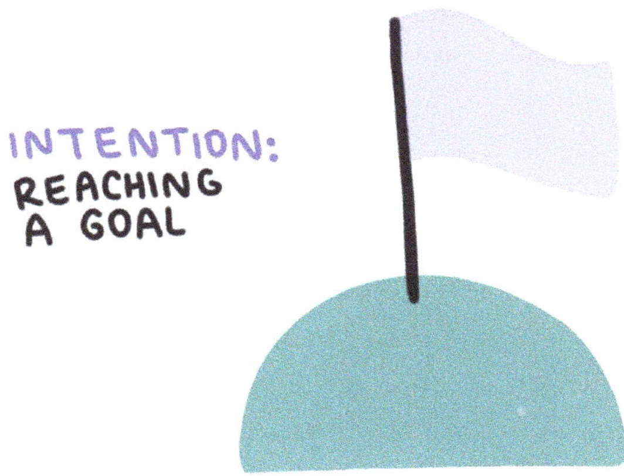

Overlapping and Intertwining

When you sketchnote, you're using your visual language and your written language together to communicate meaning. And you can unite these two languages even more smoothly by overlapping and intertwining them.

Overlapping and intertwining are completely optional. They're just more nuanced ways of grouping elements and information without keeping everything individual/static. In other words, they help bring your sketchnote to life.

These techniques can give you permission not to draw a whole image. You can hide part of it behind other words or graphics like I did in the examples below. It's also a great way to save space and create a unified look.

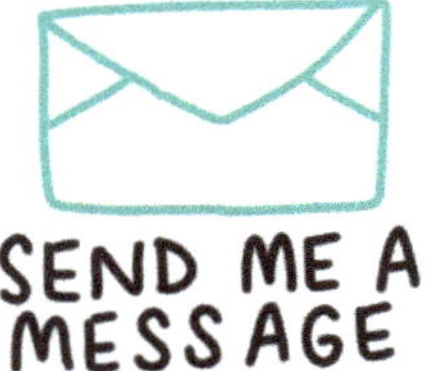

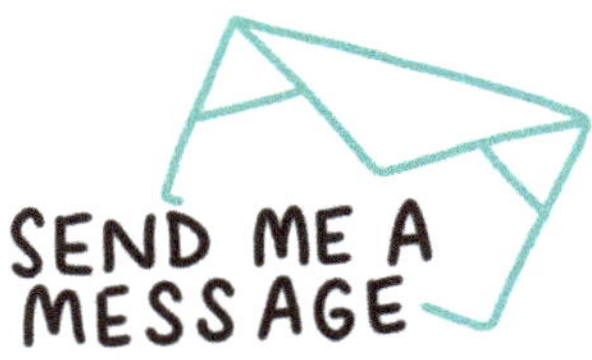

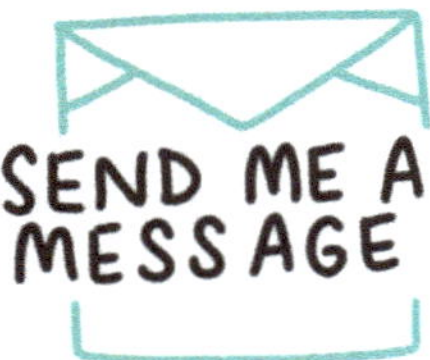

There aren't specific techniques to teach here—it's more of a general awareness of how you can use different elements together. Eventually, you'll stop thinking about *how* to do it and just start combining them instinctively!

BRINGING IT ALL TOGETHER

Now that we've explored the act of sketchnoting as well as the parts of a sketchnote, it's time to bring it all together and finish it off. Here are a few things to do or consider as you wrap up your sketchnote—and when you're planning the next one!

Last-Minute Questions to Make Your Sketchnote Clearer

When you're close to completing your sketchnote, take one last look at it and make sure that you've recorded everything you need to in a way that you'll understand when you come back to it later.

- ☑ Are there any final connections that you need to make or clarify?

- ☑ Did you miss a piece of content that's important to capture before you forget?

- ☑ Do you need to highlight something so that it stands out as extra important when you refer to it later?

- ☑ Are you running out of space and need to jot something down on a piece of paper for later?

- ☑ Is there anything you can add that would enhance the flow of your sketchnote?

Take a look at the sketchnote and see if you missed anything. As this is *your* learning tool, you need to make sure that everything works for you and will be clear when you come back to review it later.

Unify Lists With Bullets

Bullets are great for adding visual pizzazz to lists or groups of information. Using matching bullet points can also show that information belongs together. Some of my go-to bullet drawings are simple dots, diamonds, or squares, but you can jazz them up depending on how much time you have!

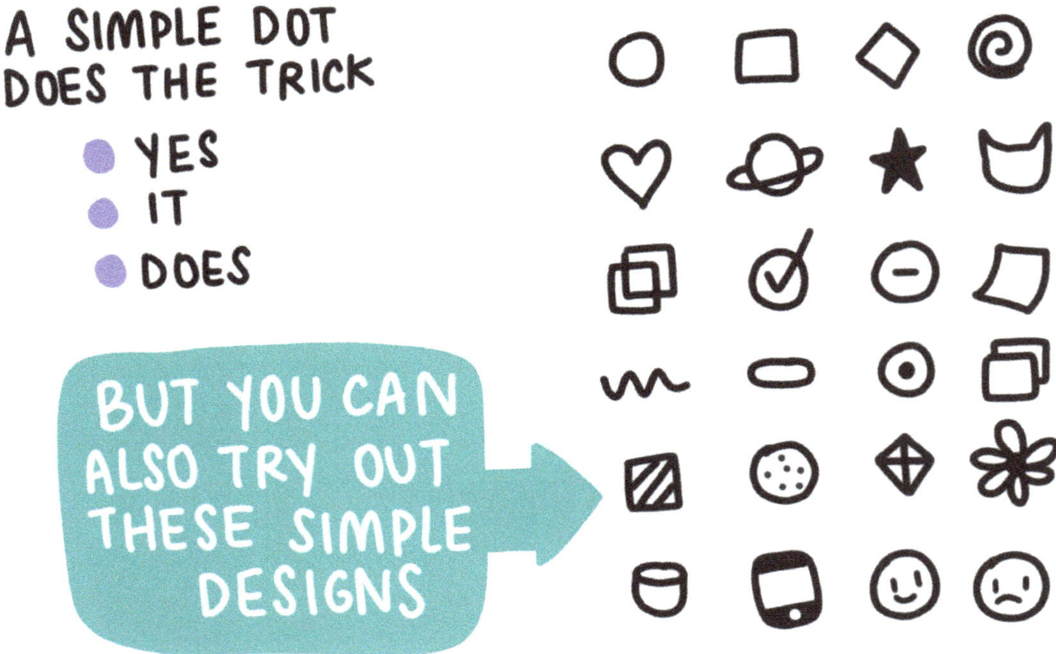

Consider Adding Some Shadows

Shadows are a fun and easy way to help bring your sketchnote to life. I usually save them for the end and do them all at the same time—but you're welcome to add them when the mood strikes.

To make your shadows stand out, keep them consistent across all of your objects. Imagine a light source and visualize where that light would hit the object and where the shadow would be. Draw the shadows there. Then keep that imaginary light source the same for all the shadows you add to that sketchnote.

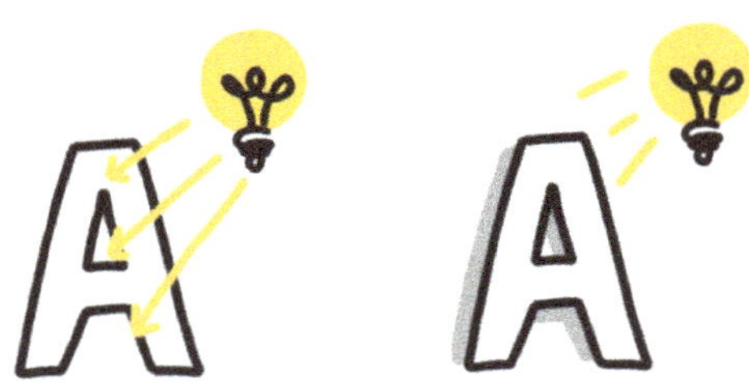

Create the Look of Completion

This is totally optional, but sometimes it's nice to draw a border around the outside of your sketchnote to represent that it's complete. If space is too tight (like if you're drawing in a small notebook), you might have to think about this ahead of time so that you don't crowd your edges.

Sign and Date Your Sketchnote

Last but not least, don't forget to sign and date your sketchnote if you didn't do it at the beginning. Ok, I guess the signature is optional, especially if you don't plan on sharing these widely, but it's still a fun way to complete your sketchnote.

Even if you're sketchnoting a one-off lecture or meeting, I recommend including the date. I've come across sketchnotes in notebooks that I'd forgotten about, and I was happy that I added the date all those years before so I could reflect on how far I'd come!

Things to Consider for Next Time

Sketchnoting is a practice, and part of that practice is learning from each attempt and applying your insights the next time you try it! Reviewing your sketchnotes is a great way to improve your skills quickly!

Here are some things to think about once you're looking at your finished sketchnote:

- Can you tell if the sketchnote has a logical flow? Would a different starting location have been clearer? Can you add anything now, at the end, that will enhance the flow?

- How many drawings did you incorporate? Would you have liked to add more? Less?

- What could you learn how to draw for next time?

- Did you like your color choices? Would different colors have been more effective? If so, what and why?

- How's your lettering? Any letters that you would like to improve?

☑ How's your spelling? Are there any words that you need to learn how to spell for future sketchnoting?

☑ Are there any overall design choices that you made that you would like to change? (Don't judge yourself about this) Is there information that belongs in a different place? Is there anything that you can do to make a stronger connection or link ideas together now (even if it makes your sketchnote look a little messier?)

And Probably the Most Common Question: Did You Run Out of Space?

This can happen and it gets easier to avoid the more you practice. Here are some strategic things you can try to help make everything fit next time.

One strategic move is dividing your page into sections before you start. If the class or presentation is an hour long, you could divide the page into quarters and fill one quarter every 15 minutes. Use very light pencil lines that can be erased easily—it's really just a guide for your use. You don't have to follow the guide perfectly but this can help you, especially when you're new to sketchnoting.

60 MINUTES:

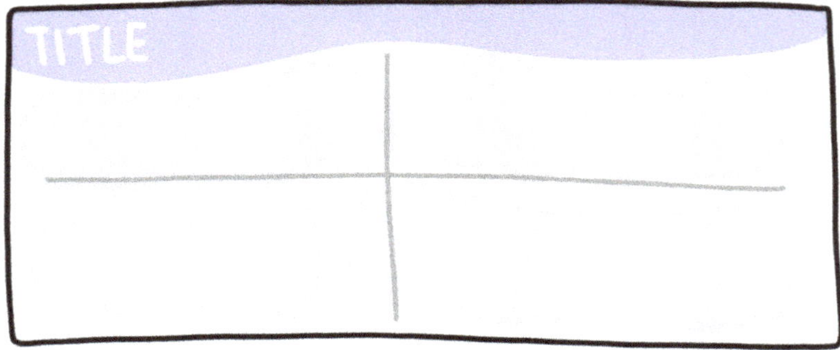

Another strategy is not committing to paper right away. Though I would highly encourage you to just put pencil to paper and start, you can hold off for a little while. For example, if the presentation or class is an hour long, you could decide to not commit to paper for the first ten minutes. You could have some scrap paper or another page in your notebook where you could jot a few notes then decide what you want to draw.

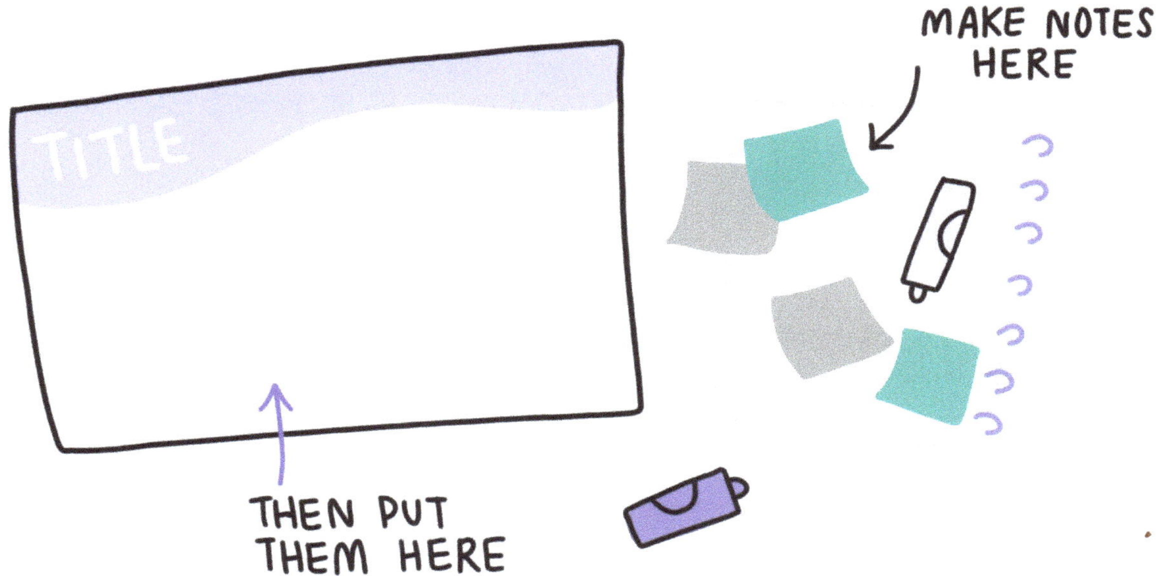

I often choose this method if the person starts their presentation with a story and I'm not sure what the conclusion of that story will be. I might make some notes about the plot and then decide if I want to capture the details or just the outcome or lesson that they finished with.

Note: it's totally okay if it doesn't all fit on one page. If you are capturing a lot, or if a session runs over, you may need more paper. That's ok! Flip to a new page or add on a piece and tape it together later.

If you're using multiple pieces of paper and you need to connect information on different sheets, get creative! Give yourself permission to rip out the pages and tape them together. Choose a color and highlight the ones that go together—create a legend for yourself if you need to!

Do whatever works best for you and try not to worry!

ONE LAST THING TO REMEMBER

Sketchnoting is a Journey, Not a Destination,

We've almost reached the end of the book—but your sketchnoting journey is just beginning. And I want to leave you with a reminder and some encouragement:

This is a process. You'll have times when you feel like you're messing up or falling behind. You won't love every sketchnote you do. I don't love every sketchnote I do, either.

If (when) you make a mistake or create a graphic you don't love, be gentle with yourself. Your goal is not to be perfect. Let me say that again: YOUR GOAL IS NOT TO BE PERFECT. Your only goal is to show up, give it a try, and learn along the way.

My Sketchnoting Journey

When I created my first sketchnote, I just wanted to apply what I had learned in the workshop I went to. It worked like a charm and I was happy with it. Here's the result:

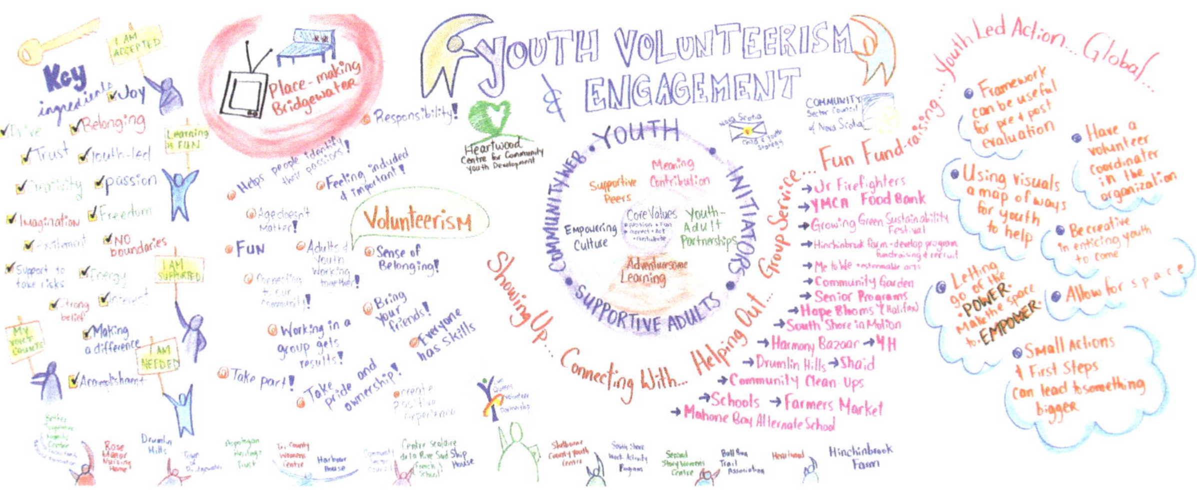

Now that you're familiar with the foundations of sketchnoting, you might be able to see some of the things I could have done better in this first attempt. I certainly can. There's no breathing space in the sketchnote, my lettering isn't consistent, and my visual vocabulary and use of flow needed work.

But you know what? That's fine.

Sure, that first sketchnote isn't perfect. Sure, it isn't the prettiest thing I've ever seen. It still worked! It captured the information in a way that helped me remember it, even months later, and really sealed the deal for me on how powerful visuals are!

Start where you are. Grab that pencil (or pen or marker) and give it a try! Even if it's messy, it's a beginning. Every sketchnote you create will help you retain the information you're capturing—and help you build your skills.

Here's a sketchnote of mine that I created years later so you can see the difference:

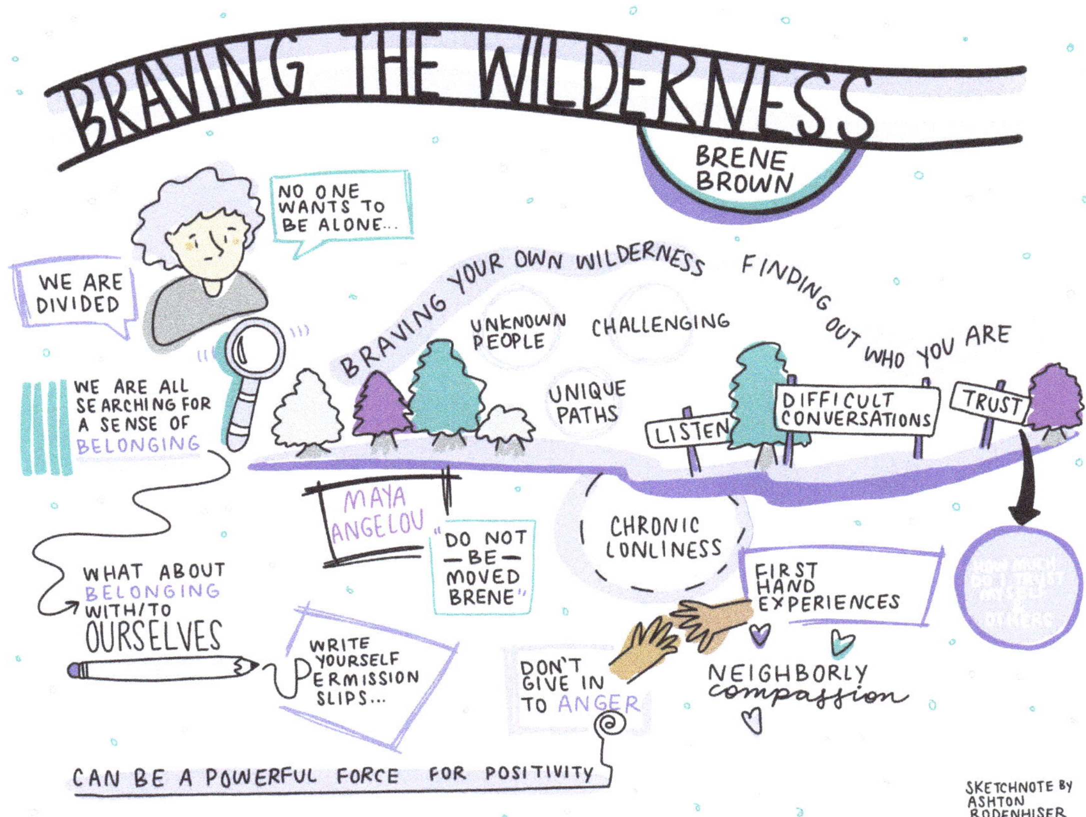

See what I mean? Know how I got better? I *practiced*. I did it over and over (and over and over and over) again. Hundreds of times. It wasn't always fun, but it was always worth it.

And you know what else? I'm not done. I'm not "perfect" (perfect is a myth). I'm always building my skills. I'm constantly looking at my notes and seeing ways I can improve them. That's how you grow. In another 10 years, I could be looking back at this example and thinking about how far I've come!

Keep going. Keep practicing. Keep trying new things. Find your own style. Find what works for you. And don't forget that you're not alone. Use #sketchnoteallthethings to share your wins and see what everyone else is up to.

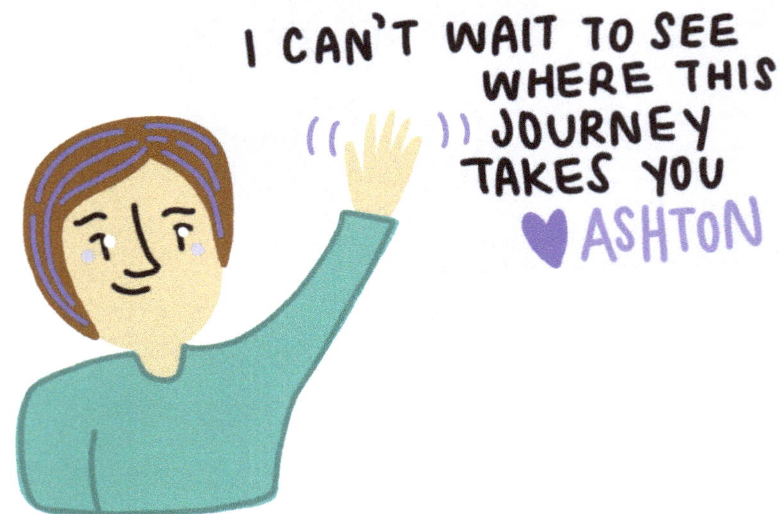

SKETCHNOTING LABORATORY: EXERCISES TO TRY

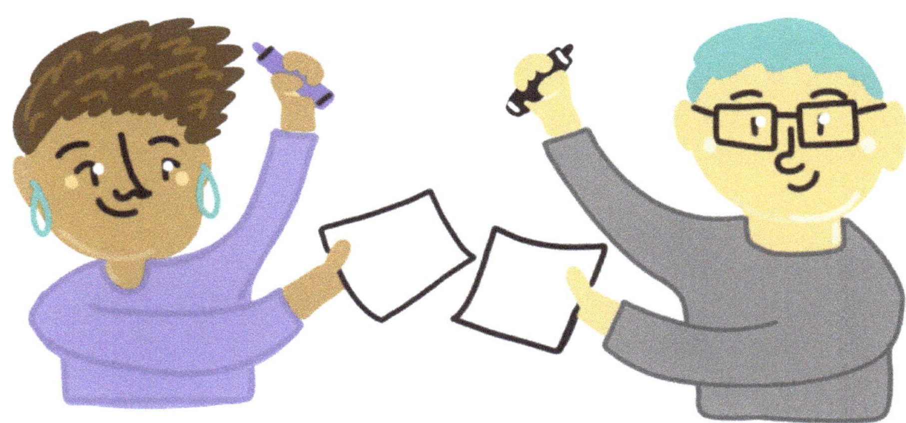

At the end of the day, the best way to get comfortable sketchnoting ... is to practice sketchnoting! Now that you've learned the elements that go into a sketchnote and some tips and tricks for listening, making sense, and capturing, it's time to PLAY!

Here are 12 things to try sketchnoting (try each one more than once!):
1. A TED or TEDx talk
2. A news broadcast
3. A documentary
4. Talk radio interview
5. Podcast
6. Webinar
7. Informational YouTube video
8. Work or board meeting
9. A chapter from a non-fiction book (audiobooks are great!)
10. A short story
11. A recipe
12. A day of your vacation

Refer to this list for inspiration while you're trying the exercises in this section. Remember: inspiration is everywhere!

Exercise 1: Identify the Elements

Look up a sketchnote online (or in this book) and identify the different elements you learned in part 1. Do you like how they're used? What would you do differently? Try redrawing the sketchnote in your own way!

Exercise 2: Switch Up Your Starting Points

Draw a sketchnote. Put the title in a different place than usual (Bottom, Left side, Right side, Center). Pick a different starting point. How do these changes affect your sketchnote? Do you like the result?

Bonus: Try this exercise again and make different choices. How does the result compare? Which do you like better?

Exercise 3: Go With the Flow

Draw a sketchnote and don't figure out how you want it to flow beforehand. Let yourself play and see how it ends up. Then decide on a new way to arrange the flow and re-draw it that way!

Exercise 4: Turn Down the Writing

Sketchnote something and try to capture the information in the fewest words possible. If you're using a recording, challenge yourself to sketchnote the whole thing without pausing or rewinding.

Bonus: Redraw the sketchnote and cut it down to even fewer words.

Exercise 5: Turn Up the Drawing

Sketchnote something using as many drawings as possible. Pause and look for inspiration online if you need help.

Bonus: Keep a notebook of drawings and add your new drawings to the book!

Exercise 6: One, Two, or Three (Colors)

Draw a sketchnote with just your main color. Draw a second sketchnote with a single accent color. Then try one with two. Finally, try one with three. Which do you like best?

Exercise 7: Speedy McSketchnoter

Sketchnote something while listening to it sped up! Try 1.25x to start, and increase the speed for an extra challenge! See how quickly you can capture!

Exercise 8: Make it a Series

If you're attending an ongoing series of classes or meetings and have a backlog of notes, take some time to review them.

A. Notice themes, terms, or ideas that reoccur regularly and brainstorm ways to use sketchnoting language to capture them. You can build your own custom visual vocabulary!

B. Try sketchnoting notes you wrote in a previous class or meeting. This is especially helpful if you're reviewing for a test or exam—sketchnoting your notes will help you retain more of the information you originally captured.

Exercise 9: One Video, Three Sketchnotes

Go to Youtube and choose a short video (5 - 15 minutes). Now watch the video three times:
The first time, capture the information using only written words.
The second time, only use pictures.
The third time, sketchnote the video using words + pictures.

Exercise 10: Share! Your! Sketchnotes!

Share your sketchnotes!
A. Create a sketchnote and email the finished product to the person you were listening to!
Bonus: Include their branding colors (colors from their website/logo).

B. Draw a sketchnote. Share it with someone you trust and ask them for their constructive criticism. You'll get more out of this if the person understands the value of sketchnoting, so take time to educate them a bit before showing it to them.

C. Sketchnote something and post it to one of your social media accounts.
Bonus: Tag the person you listened to and use the hashtag #sketchnoteallthethings!

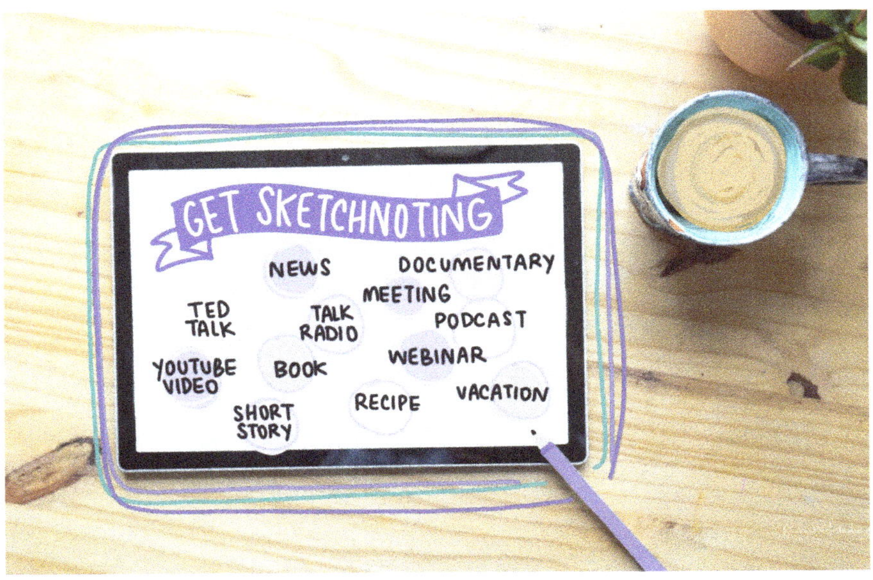

1– Improve by Sharing

In the beginning, I said don't feel pressure to share your sketchnotes (and you still don't have to) but I'm going to encourage you to do so. Get out of your comfort zone and explain your sketchnote to someone. Walk them through the process of creating it. Let the person know if you just want them to listen so you can hear yourself explain your process, or if you want feedback. If you do want feedback, describe to them what type of feedback you're looking for. If you want them to comment only on the content and not the drawings, then say so!

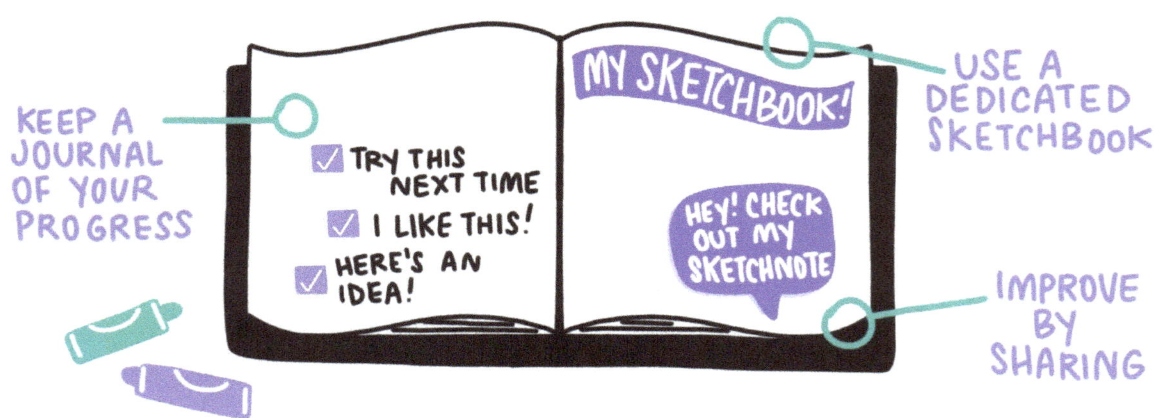

2– Use a Dedicated Sketchbook

Try keeping a dedicated sketchbook just for your sketchnoting practice. Then you can carry it with you, go back to previous drawings and ideas, redraw and get inspiration from what you've done in the past. When I was starting out, it was helpful to be able to flip back through my drawings and go, "Oh yeah! I DO know how to draw a sneaker! And here's how I did it!"

3– Keep a Journal of Your Progress

When you create a sketchnote, make a quick note in a dedicated journal about what you want to do differently on the next one. Write down any struggles that you're experiencing, observations about the process, and anything you want to try next time. You can even create a sketchnote on how you want to improve your sketchnotes!

4 – Stock up on Supplies You Love

If there's a particular pen, pencil, or marker that you love, buy it in bulk! If it's your favorite, actually use it! Often we don't use the materials we have for fear of running out and not having them anymore. Buy extra supplies that you love so that you don't fall into this trap. The same goes for notebooks.

5 – Make it Work for You

Do you find a full sheet of paper intimidating? Try sketchnoting a single topic on a post-it note or index card. Or is the opposite true—do you worry about running out of space on a full sheet of paper? Try an 11x17 sheet or plan to use two pieces of paper together.

Are you worried about keeping up? Give yourself permission to switch to the notes you're used to part way through and sketchnote your notes as part of your review. Be creative and flexible and remember that this is your process and you get to decide what works for you!

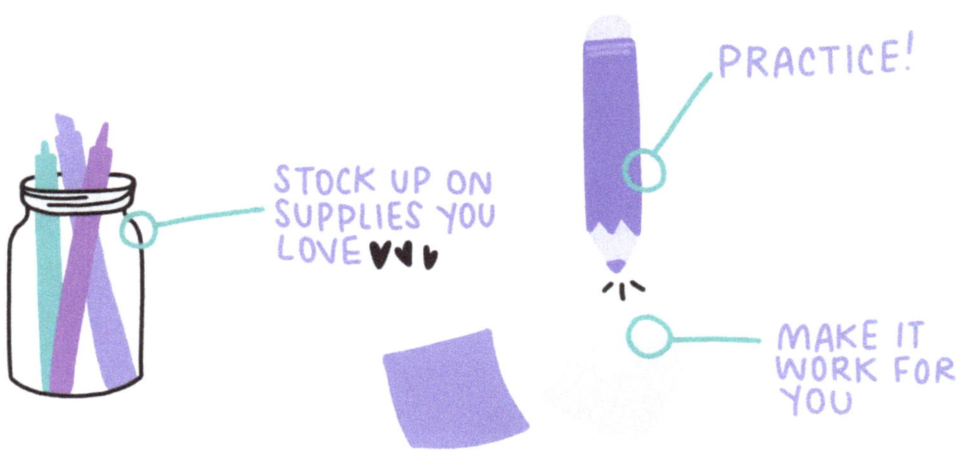

6 – Practice, Practice, Practice

If you want to improve your sketchnoting skills, you have to practice. Just like learning anything, practice makes progress. The more you sketchnote, the more confidence you'll get, and any fear, doubt, or hesitation will gently subside. Every time you listen to or watch anything, try to sketchnote it. Keep your sketchbook with you so if you find yourself in a situation where you can practice, you'll have what you need ready to go. Go back to the sketchnote laboratory exercises of this book and do them multiple times.

7 – Personality, Not Perfection!

Don't be scared to go outside the lines! The goal is NOT to create "the perfect sketchnote" (which doesn't exist!), the goal is to learn and have fun doing it! Let your colors go outside the lines! Play with shapes and flows and new images. Give yourself permission to try out different things when creating your sketchnotes and focus on the overall result, not on picky details.

8 – Be Inspired, Not Intimidated.

When checking out other people's sketchnotes, try not to allow yourself to get consumed with thoughts like, "I'll never be as good as them." The first conference I went to with other professional graphic recorders, I was so intimidated—but I chose to see them as inspiration, like, "One day maybe I'll be even half as talented as they are." If I'd let intimidation creep in, I would have barely gotten started.

9 – Reduce, Reuse, and Recycle

Sometimes my students worry about drawing the same things in multiple sketchnotes. But remember your visual vocabulary practice! Your drawings are just like words—don't be afraid to use them over and over again. This will just help solidify the graphic in your mind and body and help you in the future. Remember: it's a language!

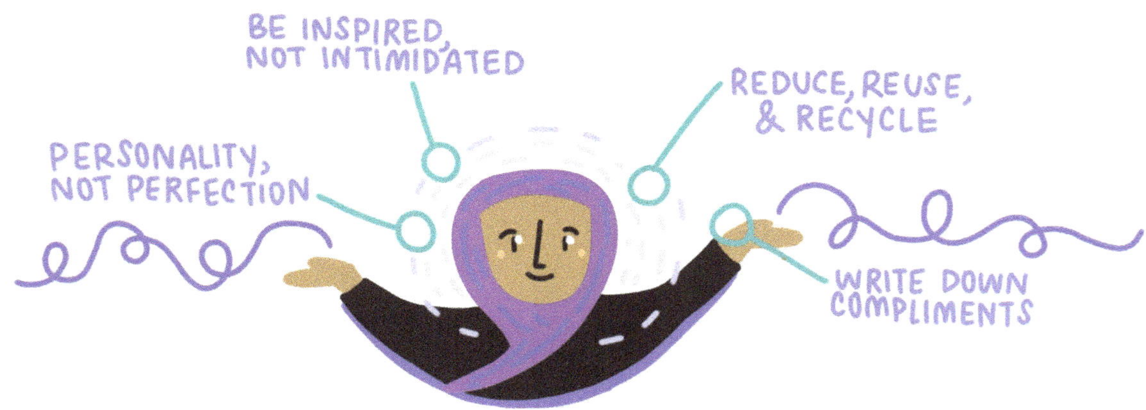

10 – Write Down Compliments

If a friend says something about your sketchnote that makes you smile, write it down! When you are starting to feel down about your ability, take out that trusty notebook and read your encouraging notes. Consider this your own personal brag sheet.

THE BEGINNER'S GUIDE TO SKETCHNOTING ONLINE RESOURCES PAGE

You may have noticed that I mentioned my online resources page many times during this book. I've packed it with all kinds of extra info and websites for you to explore, so you always have fresh inspiration at your fingertips.

"But Ashton," you may be asking, "Why do you have a website for resources when you could have listed the resources in the book?"

And yes, I could have. But I did it this way for a very specific reason:

The internet is a fast-moving place. Websites come and go. New inspiration and tools pop up all the time!

By keeping my resources online, I'm able to update these ongoing. I can add new sites that I love. I can also weed out anything that might end up obsolete or broken. This way, you're always getting my absolute favorites!

To access and download the many resources visit: www.beginnersguidetosketchnoting.com

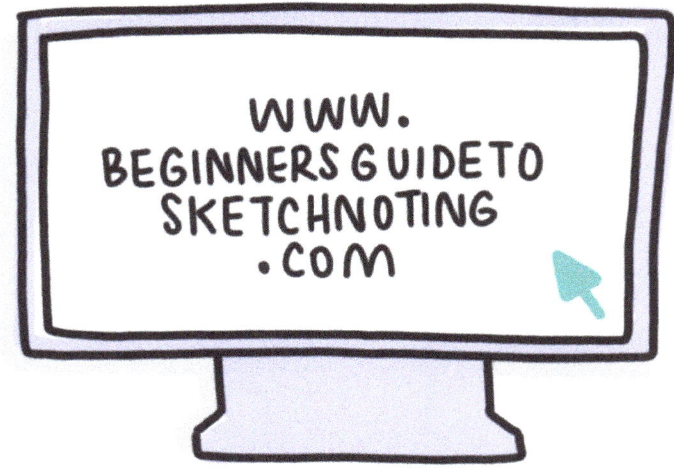

ENDNOTES

1. Agerbeck, Brandy. *The Idea Shapers: The Power of Putting Your Thinking Into Your Own Hands.* (self-pub., Loosetooth Library, 2016), 5- 26

2. Sadoski, Mark and Allan Paivio. "A Dual Coding Theoretical Model of Reading." *Theoretical Models and Processes of Reading,* 5th ed., ed. R.B. Ruddell and N.J. Unrau (Newark, DE: International Reading Association, 2013), 1329–1362.

3. Rohde, Mike. The Sketchnote Handbook, The: *The Illustrated Guide to Visual Note Taking.* (Berkeley: Peachpit Press, 2012)

4. Andrade, Jackie. "What Does Doodling Do?" *Applied Cognitive Psychology,* 24, no. 1 (January 2010): 100-106.

5. Pillars, Wendy. *Visual Note-Taking for Educators: A Teacher's Guide to Student Creativity.* (New York: Norton, 2015), 10

6. Kirkpatrick, E.A. "An Experimental Study of Memory." *Psychological Review,* 1, no. 6 (1894): 602-9.

7. Pillars, Wendy. *Visual Note-Taking for Educators: A Teacher's Guide to Student Creativity.* (New York: Norton, 2015), 53

8. Agerbeck, Brandy. *The Graphic Facilitator's Guide: How to Use Your Listening, Thinking and Drawing Skills to Make Meaning.* (self-pub., Loosetooth Library, 2012), 199

9. Lester, Paul M. "Syntactic Theory of Visual Communication." *http://paulmartinlester.info,* last modified 2006, http://paulmartinlester.info/writings/viscomtheory.html

10. Horn, Robert E. Visual Language: *Global Communication for the 21st Century.* (self-pub., MacroVU Press, 1998), (Study conducted by John Sweller)

11. Wammes, Jeffrey, Melissa Meade, and Myra Fernandes. "The Drawing Effect: Evidence for Reliable and Robust Memory Benefits in Free Recall," *The Quarterly Journal of Experimental Psychology,* 69, no. 9 (October 2015): 1-62.

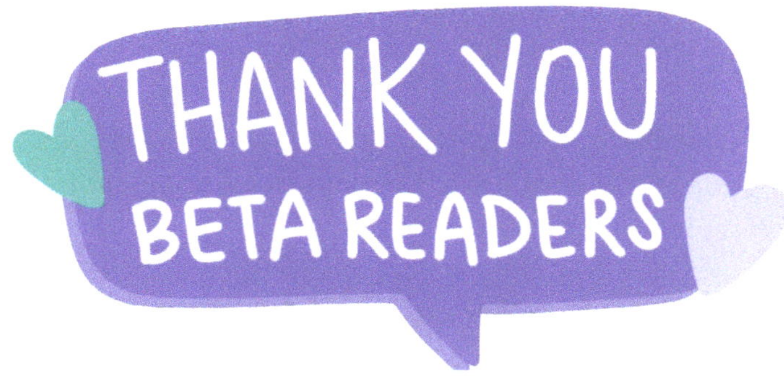

Huge thank you to all the beta readers who helped out with the development of the book!

Lauren Alexander-Binns
Alistair Hughes
Amar Asenerath
Amber Bakkum
Andrea Ruiz
Angel Jordan
Anite Robbe
Ben Reilly
Benoit Leclair
Beth Graham
Beverly Paige Wright
Brian Braganza
Brian Geddes
Chris Lewis
Debi Davis
Dhvani Doshi
Diane Salter
Emma Richard
Frank Kloeker
Lara Schroeder
Jesse Ziegler

Gregory Hadley
Janet Holmes
Jasmine Cambric
Jason Jordaan
Jaylene Chase
Jennifer Davis
Jennifer Gendron
Jennifer Santiago
Jonny Daenen
Julie Ramey
L. Elias Chan
Lindsay Foster
Bernice Williams
Lisa Kubicki
Lisa Lowthers
Chris Jarvis
Rose Kattackal
Scott Mann
Nena Snyder
Addy Strickland

Maryanne Wagstaff
Meghan Jacquot
Melissa Bogaert
Olivia Katz
Patrice Mantovani
Patsy Andersoon
Shannon Crupi
Sheila Faulstich
Sheri Kennedy
Shinesa Cambric
Susan Almon
Susan Crawford
Susana Guardado
Thomas Sihapanya
Vnay
Xiomara Mcclenton
Zainab Iqbal
Matthew Turner
Nelle Rhicard
Jesse Spangenberger

ACKNOWLEDGMENTS

I would like to express my heartfelt gratitude to Chelsea Jewell, my designer, for her exceptional patience and unwavering support. It is thanks to her dedication and guidance that this visual book has come to life in such a remarkable way.

A special thank you goes out to Meg Goodmanson, my editor, whose wisdom and assistance were instrumental in enabling me to successfully complete this book. Without her expertise and kindness, I would not have been able to achieve this significant milestone. Her contributions have been invaluable, and I am truly thankful.

The contribution of my beta readers cannot be overstated - their feedback, which amounted to over 1500 reactions across multiple iterations, has been instrumental in shaping this book into what it is today. I am deeply grateful for their time and collaboration throughout this writing journey.

I would also like to extend my heartfelt appreciation to my family, whose unwavering presence and support have been a constant source of strength throughout this process. The graphic facilitators, graphic recorders, and sketchnoters I have had the pleasure of meeting along the way have been incredible sources of inspiration and encouragement. Their willingness to lend a supportive ear over the years has meant the world to me.

I am incredibly thankful to Erin Weigel for her contribution in crafting the tagline for the book. Her creative input has added a special touch that perfectly captures its essence. Additionally, I want to express my gratitude to Rob Fitzpatrick and the Write Useful Books community for generously sharing their knowledge and patiently addressing my numerous questions throughout this journey.

To each and every person mentioned, and to all those who have played a part in this journey, I extend my deepest gratitude. Your contributions and support have made this book a reality, and I am truly honored to have had the opportunity to work with such remarkable individuals.

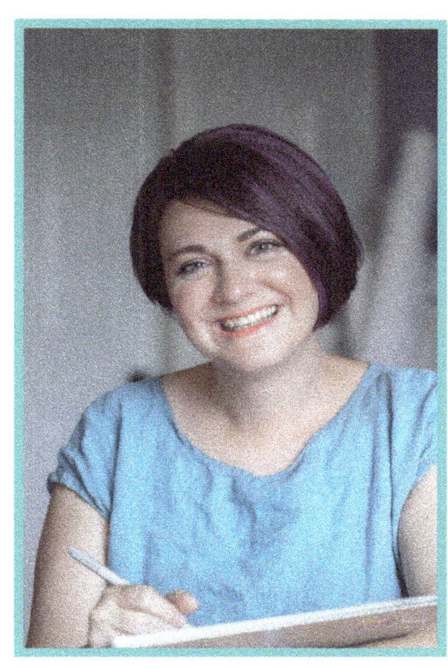

ABOUT ASHTON

Ashton Rodenhiser is an internationally acclaimed graphic recorder renowned for her sketchnoting and graphic facilitation expertise. Since 2013, she has been capturing keynotes, meetings, and seminars through visually engaging illustrations. Hailing from Canada, Ashton has collaborated with prestigious organizations such as Microsoft, Amazon, Michelin and various national and international associations.

The pivotal moment that altered Ashton's trajectory occurred in 2013 during a workshop on graphic facilitation. Inspired by the transformative techniques she was learning, she decided to pull from her passion as a creative and the skills she had developed as facilitator to launch her business, Mind's Eye Creative. Since then she's been on a mission to showcase and teach others the power of visual communication and visual thinking.

Recognizing the profound impact of sketchnoting as a tool for thinking and learning, Ashton firmly believes in its power to help others engage creatively while deepening their understanding. It's her passion to help individuals express their ideas in imaginative and compelling ways. You can find other books of hers including: *Doodle the Maritimes*, *DevOps Doodles* and *How to Draw Titles* available from her website. She teaches people all over the world in her community, Sketchnote School.